Student Workbook for Becoming an Effective Therapist

prepared by

Kim Melton
Governors State University

Len Sperry
Barry University and Medical College of Wisconsin

Jon Carlson
Governors State University

Diane Kjos
Governors State University

Boston • New York • San Francisco
Mexico City • Montreal • Toronto • London • Madrid • Munich • Paris
Hong Kong • Singapore • Tokyo • Cape Town • Sydney

For related titles and support materials, visit our online catalog at www.ablongman.com

ISBN 0-205-38167-7

Printed in the United States of America

10 9 8 7 6 5 4 3 2 1   07 06 05 04 03 02

Table of Contents

Introduction

The text *Becoming an Effective Therapist* provides comprehensive coverage of the four stages of effective therapy: engagement, assessment, intervention, and maintenance/termination. The book was designed to help therapists in training, as well as beginning therapists, to learn to practice effectively. The student handbook and accompanying student video are designed to extend your learning. By reading the book and interacting with the student handbook and video you can develop a meaningful understanding of the important strategies. Through this learning process you will learn how to use your knowledge as an instrument to help others.

We suggest that you begin your learning of each step in the therapy process by reading the chapter in the textbook and then doing the activities in the student handbook. Each section in the video is tied to a specific chapter. We wish you success on your journey toward becoming an effective therapist.

1

The Effective Therapist

Learning Objectives

■ *An integrative review of the four traditional orientations or perspectives in counseling and psychotherapy: psychodynamic, cognitive-behavioral, humanistic, and systemic.*

■ *A clinical description of the four basic "curative" factors in psychotherapy: client resources; therapeutic relationship; therapeutic intervention strategies and tactics; and faith, hope, and expectancy.*

■ *An overview of the four phases of the counseling and psychotherapy process: engagement, pattern assessment, pattern change, and maintenance/termination.*

■ *An introduction to the emerging integrative-multicultural-accountability perspective.*

Chapter Outline

I.   Four Traditional Perspectives in Psychotherapy
   A. Psychodynamic
   B. Cognitive-behavioral
   C. Humanistic
   D. Systemic

II. Integrative-Multicultural-Accountability Perspective
   A. Focus on accountability
   B. Focus on sensitivity to cultural factors
   C. Move toward integration

III. Curative Factors and Dynamics in Psychotherapy
   A. Client resources
   B. Therapeutic relationship

     C. Intervention strategies and tactics

     D. Faith, hope, and expectancy

  IV. Four Phases of the Psychotherapy Process

     A. Engagement

     B. Assessment

     C. Intervention

     D. Maintenance/Termination

Key Concepts

1. Psychotherapy can be viewed from five perspectives—psychodynamic, cognitive-behavioral, humanistic, systemic, and integrative-multicultural-accountability. Within these perspectives, it is useful to look at the therapeutic focus, therapeutic relationship, and process through which change occurs.

2. The integrative-multicultural-accountability perspective is an adaptation to a changing world. This "psychotherapy for a new millennium" addresses factors such as changes in corporations and social institutions, privatization, and the phenomenon of managed behavioral health care.

3. A commonality exists among the various perspectives of psychotherapy. There is a trend toward a therapeutic relationship based on collaboration and using desensitization as a common mechanism to explain a variety of therapeutic interventions.

4. While therapists have traditionally emphasized the use of a variety of specific techniques in the practice of psychotherapy, research shows that client resources are the most important influence on the outcome of therapy. The four curative factors of psychotherapy are client resources; relationship; intervention strategies and tactics; and faith, hope, and expectancy.

5. In terms of the four curative factors, client resources refer to the inner and outer resources that the client brings into therapy, which aid in recovery irrespective of the treatment process. Relationship refers to the necessary therapeutic dynamics present in a client-therapist relationship (including Carl Rogers' core conditions of effective treatment). Intervention strategies and tactics include specific methods or techniques used by the therapist based on theoretical orientation. Faith, hope, and expectancy refer to the extent to which clients believe in their therapist and believe that therapy can make a difference in their lives. Expectations for how, when, and why change will occur also contribute to effectiveness.

6. There are four phases in the process of psychotherapy: engagement, assessment, intervention, and maintenance/termination. The goal of the engagement phase is to develop a therapeutic relationship and maximize the client's readiness for change. The goal of the assessment phase is to specify the client's maladaptive pattern. The goal of the intervention phase is to modify the client's maladaptive pattern into a more adaptive pattern. The goal of the maintenance/termination phase is to maintain new, adaptive patterns and reduce or eliminate the client's reliance on the treatment relationship.

Learning Exercises

Exercise 1: A Case In Review

Laura is a 37-year-old woman who you are seeing for the first time. She is currently going through a difficult divorce and has two children. During your first session you learn that Laura feels as though she has to be perfect—she wants very much to be successful, productive, and to please other people. Laura is self-critical and works hard to organize and plan her life so as to avoid making mistakes. She would like to be a better mother, a better friend, and a better family member. Laura would also like to be more "selfish" so that she can allow herself to take care of her own needs first.

Psychodynamic Perspective

1. From a psychodynamic perspective, what would be your therapeutic focus?

_____

_____

_____

_____

2. What would your relationship with Laura be like?

_____

_____

_____

_____

3. How would you go about creating change?

_____

_____

_____

_____

4. Discuss any specific intervention techniques you might use in working with Laura from a psychodynamic perspective.

_____

_____

_____

_____

Cognitive Behavioral Perspective

5. From a cognitive behavioral perspective, what would be your therapeutic focus?

_____

_____

_____

_____

6. What would your therapeutic relationship with Laura be like?

_____

_____

_____

_____

7. How would you go about creating change?

_____

_____

_____

_____

8. Discuss any specific intervention techniques you might use in working with Laura from a cognitive-behavioral perspective.

_____

_____

_____

_____

Systems Perspective

9. From a systems perspective, what would be your therapeutic focus?

_____

_____

_____

_____

10. What would your therapeutic relationship with Laura be like?

_____

_____

_____

_____

11. How would you go about creating change?

_____

_____

_____

_____

12. Discuss any specific intervention techniques you might use in working with Laura from a systems perspective.

_____

_____

_____

_____

Humanistic Perspective

13. From a humanistic perspective what would be your therapeutic focus?

_____

_____

_____

_____

14. What would your therapeutic relationship with Laura be like?

_____

_____

_____

_____

15. How would you go about creating change?

_____

_____

_____

16. Discuss any specific intervention techniques you might use in working with Laura from a humanistic perspective.

_____

_____

_____

Integrative-multicultural-accountability Perspective

17. From an integrative-multicultural-accountability perspective, what would be your therapeutic focus?

_____

_____

_____

18. What would your therapeutic relationship with Laura be like?

_____

_____

_____

19. How would you go about creating change?

_____

_____

_____

_____

20. Discuss any specific intervention techniques you might use in working with Laura from an integrative-multicultural-accountability perspective.

_____

_____

_____

_____

Exercise 2: Understanding Your Perspective

1. Think about your responses. Which perspective are you most comfortable with? Why?

_____

_____

_____

_____

2. List some of your beliefs and values as they pertain to the process of psychotherapy.

_____

_____

_____

_____

3. How well does your particular belief system fit with each of the perspectives?

_____

_____

_____

_____

Exercise 3: Group Discussion

1. Discuss your responses to the above items. What are some differences and similarities between your belief system and that of your classmates? How much do you think a therapist's theoretical perspective affects the outcome of therapy?

2. Discuss the changing face of psychotherapy. What are some common trends visible in psychotherapy today? How do these differ from traditional psychotherapy?

3. Discuss the impact of behavioral managed health care. How will behavioral managed health care continue to affect the therapeutic process in the future?

4. Discuss the four curative factors in psychotherapy. How much does each factor affect the outcome of therapy? What are some other factors that may contribute to treatment outcomes not listed in the chapter?

5. How might a therapist move a typical client through the four phases of the counseling process? What are some factors that might interfere with the flow of therapy? How important is flexibility in the process of psychotherapy?

Chapter Quiz

True and False Questions

T F 1. Managed behavioral health care is a phenomenon of the past. Current psychotherapy methods are no longer impacted by this phenomenon.

T F 2. An integrating theme present in most forms of psychotherapy today is an expert-novice approach to the therapeutic relationship.

T F 3. Schemas organized around a traumatic childhood are present and active later in life.

T F 4. Schemas used to assist an individual in decisions between two motives are called role schemas.

T F 5. In Weiss's psychoanalytic approach to psychotherapy, the therapist takes a neutral stance.

T F 6. Processes involved in creating change in traditional psychoanalysis include confrontation, clarification, interpretation, and working through.

T F 7. Desensitization through cognitive restructuring is a method of therapeutic change used by many humanistic theorists.

T F 8. Death, meaninglessness, and isolation are the primary concerns of the existential therapist.

T F 9. Well-known family system theorists include Satir, Bowen, and Foley.

T F 10. Optimal engagement is not a necessary condition for therapy to begin, but should be reached before therapy is terminated.

T F 11. Diagnostic techniques are often employed during the assessment phase of psychotherapy.

T F 12. The severity of a client's symptoms is directly related to the client's level of functioning.

Multiple Choice Questions

1. Which therapeutic perspective focuses on dysfunctional patterns, boundaries, power, intimacy, and skill deficits?

a. Psychodynamic
b. Cognitive-Behavioral
c. Experiential
d. Systems

2. In which theoretical perspective is the focus on the discrepancy between real and ideal self-schemas and the disturbance in boundaries between the self and others?

a. Psychodynamic
b. Cognitive-Behavioral
c. Experiential
d. Integrative-multicultural-accountability

3. Which statement best describes the therapeutic change process based on the Cognitive-Behavioral perspective?

a. Confrontation, clarification, interpretation, and working through
b. Desensitization through various forms of exposure therapy or restructuring
c. Facing fear of life's ultimate concerns
d. All of the above

4. Which best describes the Horowitz (1988) theory of schemas within the psychoanalytic perspective?

a. Multiple schemas of self and other include self-schemas, innovational schemas, role schemas, value schemas, and superordinate schemas.
b. A two-part schema model exists, consisting of the ego and sequestered schema.
c. Types of schemas such as cognitive, affective, motivational, instrumental, and control schemas are present.
d. None of the above.

5. In the course of treatment, what percentage of improvement can be attributed to client resources?

a. 50%
b. 25%
c. 40%
d. 15%

6. In the course of treatment, what percentage of improvement can be attributed to intervention strategies and tactics?

a. 50%
b. 25%
c. 40%
d. 15%

7. What are the conditions that Carl Rogers described as the core conditions of effective counseling?

a. Caring, respect, and cooperation
b. Empathy, respect, and genuineness
c. Kindness, understanding, and respect
d. Empathy, kindness, and understanding

8. Lambert proposed that therapists focus on

a. specific interventions, tactics, and techniques.
b. understanding, listening, encouraging, and building relationships.
c. developing a common language between therapist and client.
d. educating the client by presenting useful data to aid in the recovery process.

9. Which curative factor is most influenced by the placebo effect?

a. Client resources

b. Relationship

c. Intervention strategies and tactics

d. Faith, hope, and expectancy

10. Readiness for change is first assessed during which phase of the counseling or psychotherapy process?

a. Engagement

b. Assessment

c. Intervention

d. Maintenance/termination

11. What is the goal of the intervention phase of the counseling or psychotherapy process?

a. To decrease symptoms

b. To increase life functioning

c. To modify maladaptive patterns

d. Both a and b

e. All of the above

12. What methods are used in the maintenance and termination phase of the counseling or psychotherapy process?

a. Terminating therapy and medication abruptly so the client can quickly adjust to life without therapy.

b. Maintaining the client's reliance on therapy so as to prevent relapse.

c. Referring the client to a new therapist to continue with the cycle of psychotherapy.

d. Schedule weaning sessions, negotiate a termination date, and increasingly space medication maintenance sessions.

2
Engagement

Learning Objectives

- *Characteristics of sufficiently engaged clients compared to clients who are not sufficiently engaged in the treatment process.*

- *Seven therapeutic intervention skills for fostering client engagement in therapy.*

- *Five stages of readiness for change and methods of optimizing readiness for change.*

- *The meaning and value of the client's explanatory model and expectations for treatment in fostering engagement and in planning treatment.*

- *The value and methods for negotiating the focus and goals of treatment.*

- *The importance of reversing demoralization and triggering the placebo effect in the early phase of treatment.*

Chapter Outline

I. Characteristics of Client Engagement
   A. Characteristics of engaged clients
   B. Characteristics of non-engaged clients
   C. Possible reasons for non-engagement
II. Motivation for Therapy: Some Background Information
   A. Schoefield and YAVIS
III. Seven Skills for Fostering Client Engagement in Therapy
   A. Providing empathetic understanding and responding
   B. Optimizing client's level of readiness for change
      1. Five stages
         a. Precontemplation

    b. Contemplation

    c. Preparation

    d. Action

    e. Maintenance

  2. The clinical utility of motivation and readiness for change: implications for psychotherapy practice

C. Exploring client's explanatory models

D. Eliciting client's expectations for treatment

E. Negotiating mutually agreeable treatment focus and goals

F. Reversing client's demoralization

G. Triggering the placebo effect

Key Concepts

1. Client's motivation or stage of readiness for change is a better predictor of treatment outcome than factors such as age, problem severity, socioeconomic status, self-esteem, or social support network.

2. Engagement is the first and most important phase in the treatment process. Engagement is essential for therapeutic change to occur.

3. There are several differences between characteristics of engaged clients and characteristics of non-engaged clients. The primary differences involve empathy, treatment goals and focus, treatment outcomes, hopefulness, confidence in treatment, and level of readiness for change.

4. Five stages of readiness for change have been identified. However, movement through these stages is sometimes bi-directional.

5. A client's explanatory model must be somewhat aligned with the therapist's case formulation for effective change to occur.

6. The client's expectations of therapy and of the therapist are strong predictors for the outcome of therapy. Effective therapists will explore these expectations.

7. Educating clients about the process of psychotherapy often results in fewer premature terminations and more positive treatment outcomes.

8. Reversing demoralization is a continuous process. Therapists can offer empathy, hope, and reassurance to foster remoralization in clients.

9. It is possible to trigger or enhance the placebo effect in clients. Therapists can do so by attending to the client, expressing interest and concern for the client, presenting a professional manner, and expressing confidence in the treatment plan and outcomes.

Learning Exercises

Doug, 27, is seeing you for the first time at the request of his girlfriend, with whom he has a one-year-old daughter. Doug has been unable to keep a job for more than a three month period. He feels tired all of the time and often misses work because he is unable to get out of bed. Despite the fact that Doug's physician has found no physical cause for his symptoms, Doug is convinced that his problem is biological in nature. Doug's inability to hold a job and to contribute financially has caused a great deal of strain on his relationship. As a result, Doug has recently moved from the apartment he shared with his girlfriend and daughter to his parents' home. Doug would like to get his life together so that he can reconcile with his girlfriend. He is not sure how therapy will help but is willing to give it a shot.

Exercise 1: Providing Empathetic Understanding: Seeing the World Through the Client's View.

1. Imagine that you are Doug. What emotions would you feel?

_____

_____

_____

_____

2. List at least ten words to describe these feelings.

_____

_____

_____

_____

3. What thoughts would you experience?

_____

_____

_____

_____

4. How would your current situation affect your self-concept?

_____

_____

_____

_____

5. How would your current situation affect your worldview?

_____

_____

_____

_____

6. What would your attitude be toward therapy?

_____

_____

_____

_____

Exercise 2: Optimizing Client's Level of Readiness for Change

1. At what stage of readiness for change do you think Doug is currently functioning? Why?

_____

_____

_____

_____

2. What are some factors in Doug's life that might act as barriers to the change process?

_____

_____

_____

_____

3. As Doug's therapist, how might you tailor your treatment to his stage of readiness for change?

_____

_____

_____

_____

4. List at least three interventions for optimizing a client's readiness for change.

_____

_____

_____

_____

5. As your therapy with Doug continues, what are other interventions that might assist him in his journey toward change?

_____

_____

_____

_____

Exercise 3: Exploring Client's Explanatory Model

1. What does Doug believe to be the source of his problem?

_____

_____

_____

2. Based on your first few sessions with Doug, you believe his symptoms are largely due to depression. How would you help Doug to understand his problem through a wider lens?

_____

_____

_____

_____

Exercise 4 & 5: Eliciting a Client's Expectations for the Treatment Process/Treatment Outcomes and Negotiating Mutually Agreeable Treatment Focus, Goals, and Outcomes.

1. Doug mentions that he doesn't see how therapy will work but he is willing to "give it a shot." How might you elicit Doug's expectations for treatment (symptom relief, improvement in functioning, personality change, modality of treatment, and treatment methods)?

_____

_____

_____

_____

2. How would you describe your role, as a therapist, in the treatment process?

_____

_____

_____

_____

3. How could you help Doug to define his role and responsibilities?

_____

_____

_____

_____

4. Doug mentions that his only goal is to appease his girlfriend so that he can move back into their apartment. He believes that by merely attending therapy sessions he will accomplish this goal. You believe that Doug must first work on himself (i.e., deal with his depression) before he can work on his relationship. You would like Doug to look internally rather than to simply focus on external solutions. How might you work with Doug to better align your treatment goals and expectations?

_____

_____

_____

_____

Exercise 6 & 7: Reversing Demoralization and Triggering the Placebo Effect

1. In what ways might Doug feel demoralized?

_____

_____

_____

_____

2. How would you help him to feel remoralized?

_____

_____

_____

_____

3. List some therapist characteristics that might aid in the process of remoralization.

_____

_____

_____

_____

4. How might you trigger the placebo effect in your therapy with Doug?

_____

_____

_____

_____

5. How would this benefit the therapeutic process?

_____

_____

_____

_____

Video Exercises

A. Watch the following video segment of Jill and David Scharff working with Judy, Pam, and Adrian.

1. What did you notice about this video segment? What are your initial reactions?
2. How do Adrian's (the father) comments define his role in this session?
3. How do Adrian's comments define his wife's (Judy) role in the session?
4. How does Adrian define his daughter's (Pam) role in the session?
5. How do you think this sets up the role of the therapist in this session?

B. Watch the following video segment as Jill and David Scharff continue to work with Judy, Pam, and Adrian and elicit the family's explanatory model and treatment expectations.

1. What did you notice about this video segment? What are your initial reactions?
2. How does David Scharff elicit Pam's understanding of the family's problem?
3. What is Pam's explanation for the family's problem?
4. How does David Scharff elicit the clients' expectations or goals for therapy?
5. What does Judy suggest as the family's goals for therapy?
6. What else did you notice in this segment?

C. Watch the following video segment as Jill and David Scharff demonstrate the use of empathetic responding skills.

1. What did you notice about this video segment? What are your initial reactions?
2. How effectively do you think Jill Scharff used empathy in responding to Judy?
3. Do you think Judy felt heard and understood?
4. Do you think Judy felt safe to talk about and experience the emotion she was feeling?
5. How does the use of empathy help to achieve engagement in therapy?
6. Do you think that Judy was engaged in the therapy session? Explain.

Chapter Quiz

True and False Questions

T F   1. Clients with similar presenting problems will share similar symptoms and treatment goals.

T F   2. Engagement is a necessary and sufficient factor for change to occur.

T F   3. An engaged client attends and actively participates in sessions, but does not necessarily feel understood by the therapist.

T F   4. One way to increase a client's level of engagement is to trigger the placebo effect.

T F   5. Motivation is the key to effective therapy.

T F   6. Readiness for change is a stable personality characteristic.

T F   7. The concept of readiness for change is applicable across cultures.

T F   8. Significant differences between a client's explanatory model and the therapist case formulation can result in non-adherence.

T F   9. Learned helplessness can be overcome through remoralization.

T F   10. The placebo effect always results in a better client-therapist relationship.

Multiple Choice Questions

1. Which is not a characteristic of engaged clients?

a. Confident in the therapist's ability to help
b. Has a unique view of treatment goals
c. Is hopeful about solving problems
d. Actively participates in sessions

2. Which is the most important determiner of treatment outcomes?

a. Client's expectation
b. Client's level of readiness for change
c. Client's socioeconomic status
d. Gender

3. What does the acronym YAVIS stand for?

a. Young, Attentive, Vocal, Interesting, Sensitive
b. Young, Attractive, Verbal, Intelligent, Successful
c. Young, Achieving, Verbal, Intuitive, Successful
d. None of the above

4. Which statement best describes the concept of empathy?

a. Treating the client with compassion and respect.
b. Viewing the world through the client's eyes; allowing yourself to get lost in the client's experience.
c. Understanding the client's subjective experience while remaining objective.
d. Both b and c.

5. Which is the third stage in a client's readiness for change?

a. Action
b. Contemplation
c. Preparation
d. Maintenance

6. Which stages are ideal for initiation of therapy?

a. Precontemplation/contemplation
b. Contemplation/preparation
c. Preparation/action
d. All of the above

7. During which stage of a client's readiness for change does the client's perception of the problem begin to look like the therapist's perception of the problem?

a. Precontemplation
b. Contemplation
c. Preparation
d. Action

8. Which intervention is appropriate for a client in the contemplation stage of readiness for change?

a. Explore the client's explanatory model.
b. Provide education and information.
c. Join with the client's ambivalence to action with a 'go slow' directive.
d. Elicit details of the client's successful efforts.

9. Which statement is most accurate regarding explanatory models?

a. The client's personal interpretation of the problem need not be shared with the therapist.

b. The client's explanatory model must match that of the therapist before therapy can commence.

c. Discrepancies between the client's explanatory model and the therapist's case formation are trivial if a client has a high readiness for change.

d. None of the above.

10. Which statement is most accurate?

a. Remoralization is to hope as placebo effect is to faith.

b. Remoralization is to faith as placebo effect is to hope.

c. Placebo effect is to positive outcomes as remoralization is to negative outcomes.

d. Placebo effect is to negative outcomes as remoralization is to positive outcomes.

3
Establishing the Therapeutic Relationship

Learning Objectives

- *Why engagement skills are vital to counseling effectiveness.*

- *Attending and joining skills including internal attending, physical attending, and verbal attending, and how these skills are effectively used.*

- *Active listening skills including minimal prompts, reflecting content, and reflecting feelings, and when and how these skills contribute to the engagement process.*

- *Encouragement skills and their contribution to a positive therapy outcome.*

Chapter Outline

I. Engagement Skills
   A. Attending and joining skills
      1. Internal
      2. Physical
      3. Verbal
   B. Active listening skills
      1. Minimal prompts
      2. Reflecting content
      3. Reflecting feeling
      4. Appropriate use of silence
   C. Empathetic responding skills
      1. Adding feeling and meaning to client's message
      2. Communicating caring, respect, and understanding

D. Encouragement skills
    1. Verbal and nonverbal encouragement
    2. Marking behaviors
    3. Eliciting positives

Key Concepts

1. Attending and joining skills are essential to effective engagement and are actively utilized throughout the process of counseling and psychotherapy. These skills include internal, physical, and verbal attending. The purpose of attending and joining skills is to communicate interest, caring, and understanding to the client.

2. Active listening skills are used to elicit client stories. These skills help clients feel as though they are truly being heard and understood, and act as a gentle guide that provides security and direction. Active listening skills include using minimal prompts, reflecting content, reflecting feeling, and use of silence.

3. Empathetic responding skills combine attending and joining skills with active listening skills. Together, these skills enable the counselor to hear and communicate to the client the feelings and the underlying meaning of what the client is and is not saying. These skills also help the counselor to understand the message that the client is communicating. As a result the client feels safe, appreciated, and understood.

4. Counselors encourage clients by helping them identify their personal strengths. By encouraging clients both verbally and nonverbally, therapists empower clients and help them to share and to trust. Encouragement can also be used to impact client behavior. Attending to a client's positive behavior can encourage future productive behavior.

Learning Activities

Exercise 1: Exercises in Attending and Joining

Consider the following exchange between two friends.

Michelle: Mary, can we talk for a few minutes?

Mary: Sure, is something bothering you?

Michelle: Well, yes. Are you sure you have time to listen?

Mary: Of course I do. What else are friends for?

Michelle: Okay. Well, it's just that lately I've been feeling really stressed out.

Mary: *You've* been feeling stressed? Did I tell you how stressed I've been feeling lately? I'm just overwhelmed. Work has been a nightmare. Did I tell you how busy we have been at the office lately? I've been going nuts.

Michelle: Oh yeah?

Mary: Yeah. You're probably just stressed about work too. I don't blame you. After all, you've been busy these days. Don't worry. It will all pass.

1. How well do you think Michelle felt heard in this example?

_____

_____

_____

2. How do you think Michelle felt after Mary's response?

_____

_____

_____

3. Can you remember a time when you came to a friend with a problem and experienced something similar?

_____

_____

_____

4. How did you feel?

_____

_____

_____

5. Pair up with a partner in class. Rewrite the dialog between Michelle and

Mary. This time, write the example so that Mary is using the attending skills discussed in the chapter.

Michelle: Mary, can we talk for a few minutes?

Mary: Sure, is something bothering you?

Michelle: Well, yes. Are you sure you have time to listen?

Mary: Of course I do. What else are friends for?

Michelle: Okay. Well, it's just that lately I've been feeling really stressed out.

Mary:_____

_____

_____

Michelle:_____

_____

_____

Mary:_____

_____

_____

Michelle:_____

_____

_____

Exercise 2: Role-play

Role-play a similar dialog with your partner for approximately three to five minutes. Talk about a time when you felt a great deal of stress. First, choose one partner to act as the counselor while the other acts as the client. Next, switch roles. Be sure to focus on internal, verbal, and physical attending and joining skills.

1. What did you notice, as the client, when you were being attended to?

_____

_____

_____

2. What did you notice, as the counselor, as you attended to your client?

_____

_____

_____

3. How did you internally attend to your partner?

_____

_____

_____

4. How did you physically attend to your partner?

_____

_____

_____

5. How did you verbally attend to your partner?

_____

_____

_____

6. What types of nonverbal messages did your partner (client) communicate to you?

_____

_____

_____

7. What types of nonverbal messages did you communicate to your partner (client)?

_____

_____

_____

Exercise 3: Eye Contact and Nonverbal Communication—Exploring Our Comfort Levels

Eye contact can provide valuable information for the counselor or therapist. Eye contact, while subject to many cultural differences, is thought to communicate interest, attention, and respect in American culture. Each individual can tolerate different amounts of eye contact. As a counselor in training, it is important to become very comfortable with eye contact to contribute to effective attending and joining skills.

1. Pair up with your classroom partner. Situate your desks or chairs so that you and your partner can exchange the maximum amount of visual information. Set a timer or designate a timekeeper. You and your partner will maintain eye contact for exactly one minute. No verbal messages will be exchanged. Try to maintain eye contact during the entire time period. When you have finished, write your thoughts on the space provided.

_____

_____

_____

_____

_____

_____

_____

2. As you can see, eye contact is a very personal and intimate way of exchanging information. How did this exercise make you feel?

_____

_____

_____

_____

3. How comfortable were you with this exercise? Did you feel awkward? If so, why?

_____

_____

_____

_____

Exercise 4: Exercises in Active Listening, Empathetic Responding, and Encouragement

Role-play with your classroom partner. Each partner should have a chance to act as both counselor and client. Think of a situation where you felt discouraged.

Discuss this topic for approximately three minutes. The counselor will respond using only minimal prompts which include encouragers such as "uh huh" or "mhm" or simply restating the last word or words of the client's statement. Provide and exchange partner feedback and note your experiences below.

1. Did you find it difficult to use only minimal prompts?

_____

_____

_____

_____

2. Did your use of minimal prompts encourage your partner to talk?

_____

_____

_____

_____

3. How did you feel, as the client, when you were encouraged and given the space to talk freely through your counselor's use of minimal prompts?

_____

_____

_____

_____

_____

Exercise 5: Small Group Activity—Finding the Right Words

Clients often have a hard time expressing feelings. Counselors must guide clients to a greater understanding of themselves and their emotions. Active listening skills, such as reflecting feeling, require the counselor to find the right words to understand the client's experience. Terms such as mad, sad, glad, and bad are often overused as generic feeling words.

1. Get together in small groups and brainstorm words that provide a more accurate understanding of feelings and list them below.

_____

_____

_____

_____

Exercise 6: Reflecting Content, Reflecting Feeling, and Providing Encouragement Through Marking Behaviors and Eliciting Positives

Complete the following exercises by filling in effective counselor responses to the client's message.

1. "My husband wants a divorce. We have been married for twenty years and have had three children. I know things haven't been perfect, but somehow I always thought we'd work it out. I just don't know how to be me without him. I guess that is why I am here. I know I'll need some help getting through this."

Reflecting content:

_____

_____

_____

Reflecting feeling:

_____

_____

_____

Encouragement:

_____

_____

_____

2. "I've had a hard time at work lately. My boss seems to always be on my back and I feel like I can't do anything right. I keep telling myself that as long as I'm doing my best there isn't any more that I can do. Still, sometimes I'd rather just stay in bed than face another day at the office. I'm just exhausted."

Reflection of content:

_____

_____

_____

Reflection of feeling:

_____

_____

_____

Encouragement:

_____

_____

_____

3. "After six months of being sober, I just lost it. I don't know what got into me. I was feeling so depressed. I drank an entire bottle of vodka last night. My family is really disappointed. I did promise Jen that I was through with all the drinking. She really believed in me too. I was doing so well and now I've ruined it."

Reflection of content:

_____

_____

_____

Reflection of feeling:

_____

_____

_____

Encouragement:

_____

_____

_____

4. "My mother and I really had it out last night. I shouldn't have raised my voice the way I did. I know she only wants what is best for me but sometimes I feel like she still treats me like a child. I know I owe her an apology but I guess I'm embarrassed for the way I talked to her. I lost my cool."

Reflection of content:

_____

_____

_____

Reflection of feeling:

_____

_____

_____

Encouragement:

_____

_____

_____

Exercise 7: Skill Integration

Get into groups of four. Each learning pair will role-play a short session (five to eight minutes) and will then switch roles. While the first pair conducts their session, the second pair will observe and take notes of their attending skills, active listening skills, empathetic responding skills, and encouragement skills and visa versa. After each pair has completed their role-playing, provide and discuss feedback.

1. After discussing feedback with your learning partner, how well do you feel you used the beginning skills discussed in this chapter?

_____

_____

_____

_____

2. What skills do you find most difficult to use?

_____

_____

_____

_____

3. How will you improve these skills?

_____

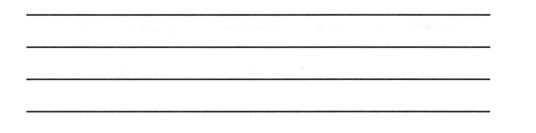

Video Exercises

A. Watch the following segment as James Bugental works with Gina and demonstrates the use of internal attending.

1. What did you notice about this segment? What are your initial reactions?
2. How effective was the internal attending activity that Bugental used?
3. What information did Bugental learn about Gina by using this internal attending activity?
4. How did the conversation following the centering activity help Bugental to understand Gina?
5. Do you think you could use a centering activity similar to the one demonstrated here? Why or why not?

B. Watch the following segment as Bugental demonstrates the use of both attending and joining skills (internal, physical, and verbal attending) and active listening skills (minimal prompts, reflecting content, reflecting feeling, and silence).

1. What did you notice in this segment? What are your initial reactions?
2. How did Bugental demonstrate the use of attending and joining skills?
3. What specific skills could you identify in this video segment?
4. How did Bugental demonstrate active listening skills?
5. What specific active listening skills could you identify in this video segment?
6. How do you think Gina felt during this segment?

C. Watch the following segment as Ken Hardy demonstrates the use of both attending and joining skills (internal, physical, and verbal attending) and active listening skills (minimal prompts, reflecting content, reflecting feeling, and silence).

1. What did you notice about this segment? What are your initial reactions?
2. How effective was Hardy's use of attending and joining skills?
3. What specific skills could you identify in this video segment?
4. How did Hardy demonstrate active listening skills?
5. What specific active listening skills could you identify in this video segment?
6. How do you think Phil (the client) felt during this segment?

Chapter Quiz

True and False Questions

T F   1. Effective engagement sets the foundation for a client's motivation for change and willingness to comply with therapy.

T F   2. Attending and joining skills can be taught and are applicable in both social and business arenas.

T F   3. Internal attending skills are beneficial and are to be used by both the therapist and the client.

T F   4. For optimal physical attending, clients should sit at opposite sides of a therapists desk, facing each other.

T F   5. Mirroring is similar to mimicking in that the therapist imitates the body language and postures of the client.

T F   6. Eye contact is a form of communication that is culture specific.

T F   7. One form of verbal attending is a therapist's use of silence.

T F   8. Minimal prompts are gentle prompts used to interrupt the client's story so that the therapist can offer feedback.

T F   9. Reflecting feeling is a good way to help clients figure out what feelings are appropriate given their situation.

T F   10. One important component of encouragement is highlighting a client's strengths.

Multiple Choice Questions

1. Which therapist spoke about "unconditional positive regard" and put great emphasis on the relationship between therapist and client?
   a. Martin Buber
   b. James Bugental
   c. Carl Rogers
   d. Virginia Satir

2. Which therapist is known for characterizing the effective therapeutic relationship as an "I-Thou" relationship?
   a. Martin Buber
   b. James Bugental
   c. Carl Rogers
   d. Virginia Satir

3. Which fundamental skills, according to the text, are considered beginning skills in psychotherapy and counseling?
   a. Active listening
   b. Attending and joining
   c. Confrontation
   d. Both a and b
   e. All of the above

4. Which statement about internal attending skills is not accurate?
   a. Internal attending skills contribute to effective engagement.
   b. Internal attending skills are used to put the therapist in a state of mind.
   c. Internal attending skills should only be used in the context of psychotherapy.
   d. Internal attending skills can be used to benefit both the therapist and the client.

5. Which is the most preferable seating arrangement for a client and therapist in a therapy session?
   a. Sitting at either side of a small desk
   b. Sitting right next to the client

c. Sitting facing each other or angled

d. None of the above

6. How do cultural differences impact the therapy session?

a. Cultural differences cloud the therapy session by preventing communication.

b. Cultural differences influence the meaning of various nonverbal forms of communication.

c. Cultural differences influence a client's expression of emotion.

d. Both b and c.

e. All of the above.

7. Which response would indicate an appropriate reflection of feeling?

a. "It sounds like you feel upset when we talk about that."

b. "If I were you, I might feel upset talking about that."

c. "I understand how you feel. I feel upset when I talk about that too."

d. None of the above.

8. Which term(s) best describes a component of silence?

a. Confrontational

b. Non-confrontational

c. Comforting

d. All of the above

9. Which statement is not an accurate description of empathy?

a. Empathy implies the ability to feel "with" another person.

b. Empathy is synonymous with sympathy.

c. Empathy involves understanding both the feeling and meaning of a client's message.

d. None of the above.

10. Which statement(s) accurately describe appropriate use of encouragement skills?

a. The therapist offers praise in response to a client's behavior.

b. The therapist elicits a client's strengths.

c. The therapist validates a client's behavior.

d. All of the above.

4
Diagnostic Assessment

Learning Objectives

- *The relationship between the assessment process and the treatment process.*

- *An introduction to three different types of assessment utilized in the context of counseling and psychotherapy: formal-diagnostic, focused-functional, and ongoing assessment or treatment monitoring.*

- *The six components and the skills of focused-functional assessment.*

- *Application of focused-functional assessment in an illustrated psychotherapy case.*

Chapter Outline

Key Concepts

1. Assessment, as discussed in this chapter, is defined as "a time-limited, formal process that collects critical information from many sources in order to reach a diagnosis, to make a prognosis, to render a biopsychosocial formulation, and to determine treatment."

2. There are four components of the assessment process: diagnosis, prognosis, biopsychosocial or clinical formulation, and treatment formulation.

3. Formal-diagnostic assessment refers to the process of collecting data about the client's current problems, functioning, and mental status, along with relevant social, developmental, and health history. The formal-diagnostic assessment also includes an assessment of the expectations and resources that a client brings to therapy.

4. Focused-functional assessment refers to the process of collecting data about a client's type and level of symptomatic distress and functional impairment. The concept of medical necessity as the basis for authorization of behavioral health care by managed care organizations comes into play for the focused-functional assessment. Treatment goals are narrowly defined and include symptom reduction and improved functioning.

5. Ongoing assessment refers to an ongoing, regular, and informal process that includes an assessment of the following: type and level of symptoms; type and level of functioning; mental status; health status; and treatment progress.

6. The formal-diagnostic assessment, which will be the focus of this chapter, includes an assessment of the following components: presenting problem and context; mental status assessment; developmental history and dynamics; social history and cultural dynamics; health history and health behaviors; and client resources.

Learning Exercises

Exercise 1: Self-Assessment

Think about your own life and the everyday stressors you encounter. Move through the components of the formal-diagnostic assessment using yourself as a client.

A. Presenting problem:

1. How might the challenges you encounter in your current life situation present themselves in a therapy session?

_____

_____

_____

_____

B. Mental status assessment:

1. Discuss your current presentation.

_____

_____

_____

2. Discuss your orientation and attitude.

_____

_____

_____

3. Discuss your mood and emotional status.

_____

_____

_____

4. Discuss your perceptual status.

_____

_____

_____

5. Discuss your cognitive status.

_____

_____

_____

6. Discuss safety factors.

_____

_____

_____

7. How do these factors influence your life functioning?

_____

_____

_____

_____

C. Developmental History and Dynamics
1. Discuss your family history.

_____

_____

_____

_____

_____

2. Describe three early childhood memories.

_____

_____

_____

_____

_____

3. What do these memories mean to you?

_____

_____

_____

_____

4. Describe yourself as a child.

_____

_____

_____

_____

5. Describe yourself now. How are you different?

_____

_____

_____

_____

6. Describe any traumatic experiences.

_____

_____

_____

_____

D. Describe your social history and cultural dynamics.
1. What is your current marital status and living situation?

_____

_____

_____

2. What is your job history and financial situation?

_____

_____

_____

_____

_____

_____

3. What are your social supports?

_____

_____

_____

_____

4. Discuss your cultural background.

_____

_____

_____

_____

_____

5. Discuss information regarding your ethnic identity, age, race, gender, sexual orientation, religion, and socioeconomic class.

_____

_____

_____

_____

_____

E. Health history and health behaviors.

1. Describe your health history and health behaviors.

_____

_____

_____

_____

_____

_____

2. List and explain any medications you are currently taking. Include both prescription and over the counter medications.

_____

_____

_____

_____

3. List and explain any medications you took regularly in the past.

_____

_____

_____

_____

4. List and explain any substances you use or have used in the past.

_____

_____

_____

_____

F. Client Resources

1. Describe your personal strengths.

_____

_____

_____

_____

_____

2. Describe your weaknesses.

_____

_____

_____

_____

3. Describe your past experiences with success.

_____

_____

_____

_____

4. Describe your past experiences with failure.

_____

_____

_____

_____

5. Explain your understanding of any current stressors or problems you are experiencing.

_____

_____

_____

_____

_____

_____

Exercise 2: Use the above information to help you in completing Skill Learning Exercises I & II, as suggested in the text

Be sure to make an audiotape of your role-play session so that you can review your performance as the therapist. Next, complete the following activities.

1. Listen to the audiotape of your role-play therapy session with your learning partner as the client and you as the therapist. What are your initial reactions?

_____

_____

_____

_____

_____

2. How well do you think you moved through the assessment process?

_____

_____

_____

_____

3. How effectively did you elicit the appropriate information for each of the components of the formal diagnostic assessment?

a. Presenting problem and context

_____

_____

_____

_____

b. Mental status

_____

_____

_____

_____

c. Developmental history and dynamics

_____

_____

_____

_____

d. Social history and cultural dynamics

_____

_____

_____

_____

e. Health history and health behaviors

_____

_____

_____

_____

f. Client resources

_____

_____

_____

_____

4. Describe your experience as the "client" in your role-play therapy session.

_____

_____

_____

_____

5. How comfortable were you during this session?

_____

_____

_____

_____

6. What was it like for you to disclose this type of personal information?

_____

_____

_____

_____

7. How can this exercise help you to understand the experience of the client in a therapy session?

_____

_____

_____

_____

Discussion Questions

1. How has the process of diagnostic assessment changed over the past few decades? Include in your discussion the effects of managed behavioral health care organization.

2. Discuss the differences between formal-diagnostic assessment, focused-functional assessment, and ongoing assessment. How are these approaches similar?

3. Discuss the components of the formal-diagnostic interview. What information should be obtained for each of these components?

4. What is involved in a mental status assessment? How might you assess each of these factors?

5. Why are cultural factors and dynamics and important components of assessment? How does an individual's culture influence what he or she brings to therapy?

Video Exercises

A. Therapists begin the formal-diagnostic assessment by gaining an understanding of the client's presenting problem. Through this process, the therapist gains a great deal of information regarding the client's current functioning. Watch the following video segment as Ken Hardy works with Phil.

1. What did you notice about this video segment? What are your initial reactions?
2. What do you see as Phil's presenting problem?
3. What questions did Hardy ask to elicit this story from Phil?
4. What aspects of Phil's life did Hardy elicit in this segment?
5. How would you assess Phil's current functioning based on this segment?
6. What aspects of Phil's life would he like to improve?
7. What are your initial reactions to this segment?
8. How effective was this initial segment of a diagnostic assessment?

B. Watch the following video segment as Jon Carlson works with Gina.

1. What did you notice about this video segment? What are your initial reactions?
2. What do you see as Gina's presenting problem?
3. What questions did Carlson ask to elicit this story from Gina?
4. What aspects of Gina's life did Carlson elicit in this segment?
5. What components of the formal-diagnostic assessment could you apply to this segment?
6. What are your initial reactions to this segment?
7. How effective was this initial segment of a diagnostic assessment?

Chapter Quiz

True and False Questions

T F   1. Over the past two decades, diagnostic assessment has become a more comprehensive and inclusive process.

T F   2. Most therapists currently use comprehensive initial clinical evaluations to get a full picture of the client's functioning.

T F   3. The current focus or goal of psychotherapy is symptom reduction and increased functioning.

T F   4. The distinction between formal-diagnostic assessment and traditional initial clinical evaluation is that the former focuses on clinical relevance during the collecting of data.

T F   5. Assessing speech abnormalities is part of the mental status assessment.

T F   6. Therapists attempt to predict or determine the likelihood that a client will commit a violent act.

T F   7. Information regarding a client's self esteem both as a child and later in life should be discussed in the section of the assessment called social history and cultural dynamics.

T F   8. Therapists should respect their clients' right to privacy by not directly asking questions regarding age or ethnic background.

Multiple Choice Questions

1. Which statement most accurately reflects the purpose of diagnostic assessment?

    a. The purpose of assessment is to match a client with specific DSM-IV criteria.

    b. The purpose of assessment is to satisfy the requirements of insurance companies so that the therapist may receive third party payments.

    c. The purpose of assessment is to assess a client's life history, worldview, and self-concept so that the therapist can devise a treatment plan.

    d. The purpose of assessment is to assess a client's symptoms, level of distress, impairment, and coping resources and to monitor a client's progress.

2. Which assessment instrument is more commonly used today in the diagnostic assessment process?

    a. The Thematic Apperception Test (TAT)

    b. The Rorschach

    c. Beck Depression Inventory

3. How is formal-diagnostic assessment different from the traditional initial evaluation?

    a. A traditional initial evaluation is more exhaustive in terms of the client's story.

    b. A traditional initial evaluation might take place over the first three sessions.

    c. A traditional initial evaluation is more focused and goal oriented.

    d. Both a and b.

4. The formal diagnostic interview includes the following:

    a. Presenting problem, mental status, relationship history, developmental history, and health history.

    b. Presenting problem, mental status, relationship history, social, history, cultural history, health history, and client resources.

    c. Presenting problem, mental status, developmental history and dynamics, social and cultural history, health history, and client resources.

    d. Presenting problem, developmental history, social history, cultural history, health history, client resources, and readiness for change.

5. An assessment of the client's presenting problem elicits which type(s) of information?

    a. Concerns that brought the client into therapy.

    b. Why the client chose this particular time in his or her life to seek therapy.

    c. How the client's concerns are influencing his or her functioning.

    d. Both a and b.

    e. All of the above.

6. Which of the following is not assessed during the mental status assessment?

    a. Orientation and attitude

    b. Relational status

    c. Perceptual status

    d. Safety

7. Which element(s) of culture is often not addressed at all by most therapists?

    a. Religion

    b. Socioeconomic status

    c. Country of origin

    d. None of the above

    e. All of the above

8. An assessment of a client's health history and health behavior must include:

    a. Prescription medication use, over the counter medication use, supplement use, and substance use.

    b. Health conditions, surgeries, and medical treatments.

    c. Attitude toward use of medication.

    d. Both a and c.

    e. All of the above.

5

From Diagnostic Assessment to Formulation and Intervention

Learning Objectives

▪ *The meaning and importance of "case formulation" and the three different types of formulations: diagnostic, clinical, and treatment formulations.*

▪ *To recognize that clients develop their own case formulations and that effective therapy requires a negotiated case formulation.*

▪ *A brief introduction to the diagnostic features of the DSM-IV.*

▪ *The skills of formulating diagnostic, clinical, and treatment formulations.*

▪ *To apply the three types of formulations in an illustrated psychotherapy case.*

Chapter Outline

I. Introduction to Case Formulation
    A. Three types of formulations
        1. Diagnostic
        2. Clinical
        3. Treatment
    B. The case formulations of clients and therapists
II. The Diagnostic Formulation
    A. DSM-IV TR and diagnostic formulation
        1. Axis I: Clinical disorders
        2. Axis II: Personality disorders or mental retardation
        3. Axis III: General medical conditions
        4. Axis IV: Psychosocial and environmental problems
        5. Axis V: Global assessment of functioning

B. Developing a diagnostic formulation

1. List all symptoms and functional impairment
2. Compare DSM-IV TR criteria
3. Specify diagnosis and Axis I, Axis II, and Axis III, if applicable
4. Fill in the information for the other axes. Specify an Axis IV designation and determine the GAF score for Axis V
5. Write a diagnostic formulation statement incorporating all five DSM Axes
6. Add a cultural formulation statement

III. The Clinical Formulation

A. Six common perspectives on clinical formulations

1. Psychodynamic
2. Cognitive-behavioral
3. Biological
4. Social
5. Adlerian
6. Integrative

B. Developing a clinical formulation

1. Specify relevant psychological factors—write brief statement
2. Specify relevant social factors—write brief statement
3. Specify relevant biological factors—write brief statement
4. Write an integrative formulation statement that incorporates the above brief formulation statements

C. Developing a treatment formulation

1. Specify targeted psychological treatment goals and treatment interventions to achieve these goals
2. Specify targeted social treatment goals and treatment interventions to achieve these goals
3. Specify targeted biological treatment goals and treatment interventions to achieve these goals
4. Write an integrative treatment formulation statement incorporating these goals and interventions

D. Case study of Juan R.

Key Concepts

1. A case formulation is a way of summarizing information about a client in a brief, concise manner for the purpose of understanding and treating the individual. There are three types of formulations—diagnostic, clinical, and treatment.

2. A diagnostic formulation is a descriptive statement that answers the question: "What happened?" It describes the client's presenting problem, symptomatic distress, and functional impairment in DSM-IV terms. To establish a diagnostic formulation the therapist goes through the following steps: identifies symptom clusters; compares these symptom clusters with DSM-IV TR criteria; specifies di-

agnoses on Axis I, II, and III; and completes information for Axis IV and Axis V, including determination of the GAF score.

3. A clinical formulation is an explanatory statement that answers the question: "Why did it happen?" It provides a rationale for the development and maintenance of the client's pattern of symptoms and impaired functioning. A clinical formulation is typically consistent with one of the following orientations: psychodynamic, cognitive-behavioral, biological, social, adlerian, or integrative. To develop a clinical formulation, the therapist specifies relevant psychological, social, and biological factors and integrates these into a formulation statement.

4. A treatment formulation is a prescriptive statement that answers the question: "What can be done about it?" It is an action plan governing treatment strategies and interventions. To develop a treatment formulation, the therapist specifies targeted psychological, social, and biological treatment goals based on the diagnostic and clinical formulations. The therapist then specifies treatment interventions to achieve these goals and writes an integrative treatment formulation incorporating the goals and interventions.

5. The greater a client's case formulation differs from the therapist's case formulation, the less likely treatment is to be effective and the more likely non-compliance will be present. The therapist must elicit the client's case formulation and begin the negotiation process to arrive at a mutually agreeable treatment direction.

6. The DSM-IV is a system that claims no adherence to a particular theoretical perspective and offers a descriptive approach to human behavior rather than an explanatory approach. Third party payers require a five axes DSM-IV TR diagnosis for approval of psychotherapy services.

Learning Activities

Exercise 1: Writing Diagnostic, Clinical, and Treatment Formulations

Consider the following case illustration of Mark. Mark is a 22- year-old, Caucasian male. After seeing Mark for the past few weeks you have gathered the following information:

Mark's troubles started very early in childhood. His mother was in and out of psychiatric institutions for some time. Her official diagnosis is unknown, although she reportedly was diagnosed with some form of schizophrenia. Mark is the youngest of two children. When Mark and his sister were very young, their mother committed suicide.

Four years later, Mark's father remarried. Mark and his sister hoped that this woman would fill the void that their mother's death had created. Instead, she was disinterested. She seemed burdened by her new husband's children, favoring her own daughter and paying very little attention to Mark and his sister. Growing up, Mark felt betrayed. He felt as if his real mother abandoned him, convinced that if he had been a better son, she would not have left him.

By the time Mark was in high school, he was acting out, running away, and coping in any way that he could. At 17 years old, Mark felt truly alone. It became apparent that Mark had some serious psychological issues and would need professional treatment. At 19 years of age, Mark admitted himself into the psychiatric unit of a community hospital. He was depressed and was feeling suicidal. During the next two years Mark was seen approximately six times as both an inpatient and an outpatient at this community mental health center. His symptoms varied, but usually he was extremely depressed and often paranoid. His symptoms seem to have prevented Mark from keeping a full time job. He had worked construction and odd jobs for the last few years.

It is unclear what diagnosis Mark had been given in the past. However, Mark reports that he has taken a variety of antipsychotic and antidepressant medications. His medications were changed quite frequently due to their disrupting side effects and his refusal to self-administer. According to Mark, no combination of medications has proven to be very effective. The therapy that he received was inconsistent, at best, and did not seem to have any beneficial effect.

Currently, Mark's symptoms of depression are evident. He often cannot sleep through the night, has very little appetite, and has lost a considerable amount of weight. Mark is also very self-critical. He has little confidence in the world around him and believes that nothing goes his way. As a result, Mark has difficulty making decisions and often cannot follow through on tasks for fear that he will fail.

Mark believes that his problems are due to the trauma he experienced early in life. He is refusing to take medication of any kind. Mark reports that he is seeking treatment at this time because he has recently moved to this area and would like to "feel better" so that he can get a full-time job. Mark's current goals include maintaining a full-time position and earning his GED.

A. Diagnostic Formulations

1. List Mark's symptoms and functional impairment.

_____

_____

2. Organize these symptoms into symptom clusters and list them below.

_____

_____

_____

_____

3. Compare these symptom clusters to DSM IV criteria. Discuss what you have determined with regards to specific diagnoses on each DSM axis.

_____

_____

_____

_____

4. Write a diagnostic formulation regarding Mark's presentation.

_____

_____

_____

_____

_____

_____

_____

_____

B. Clinical Formulations

1. Specify relevant factors contributing to Mark's psychological functioning. Write a brief psychological formulation statement.

_____

_____

2. Specify relevant factors contributing to Mark's social functioning (include cultural and family dynamics). Write a brief social formulation statement.

3. Specify relevant factors contributing to Mark's biological functioning. Write a brief biological formulation statement.

4. Write an integrative formulation statement that incorporates the above brief formulation statements.

C. Treatment Formulations

1. Specify targeted psychological treatment goals based on Mark's diagnostic and clinical formulations. Specify one intervention to achieve these goals.

2. Specify targeted social treatment goals based on Mark's diagnostic and clinical formulations. Specify one intervention to achieve these goals.

_____

_____

_____

_____

3. Specify targeted biological treatment goals based on Mark's diagnostic and clinical formulations. Specify one intervention to achieve these goals.

_____

_____

_____

_____

4. Write an integrative treatment formulation statement incorporating these goals and interventions.

_____

_____

_____

_____

_____

_____

_____

Exercise 2: Understanding Mark's Explanatory Model

1. Describe Mark's explanatory model.

_____

_____

_____

_____

2. How does your case formulation differ from Mark's? How will you address this difference?

_____

_____

_____

_____

Video Exercises

A. Watch the following segment as Arnold Lazarus discusses his view of an appropriate treatment formulation for Juan.

1. What did you notice about this segment? What are your initial reactions?
2. Does Juan accept Lazarus's version of an appropriate treatment plan?
3. Where would Juan and Lazarus go from here in order to develop an appropriate treatment formulation?

B. Watch the following video segment as Jon Carlson works with Gina to develop a possible direction for therapy.

1. What did you notice about this segment? What are your initial reactions?
2. What is it that Carlson suggests that Gina consider?
3. Does Gina accept Carlson's suggestions?
4. Where would Gina and Carlson go from here in order to develop an appropriate treatment formulation?

C. Watch the following video segment as Len Sperry works to develop a mutual understanding of Kathleen's case formulation.

1. What did you notice about this video segment? What are your initial reactions?
2. How does Sperry attempt to elicit Kathleen's case formulation?
3. What does Sperry learn about Kathleen during this segment?
4. Where would Sperry go from here in order to elicit a better understanding of Kathleen's formulation?

D. Watch the following segment as Len Sperry continues to work with Kathleen and then discusses the development of his formulation.

1. What did you notice about this segment? What are your initial reactions?
2. Why would Sperry have asked the client to demonstrate her symptoms nonverbally?
3. How was this segment useful for Sperry in the development of a case formulation?

Chapter Quiz

True and False Questions

T F   1. Formulated treatment plans must be submitted to third party payers for approval before the initiation of therapy.

T F   2. The diagnostic formulation includes a description of symptoms and functioning.

T F   3. The DSM-IV describes the symptoms related to a particular disorder and explains why treatment is necessary.

T F   4. Most clients do not come to therapy with a developed treatment formulation.

T F   5. Typically, the client and therapist have similar treatment formulations, where they differ is in treatment goals.

T F   6. The Global Assessment of Functioning is a numerical measure of a client's symptomatic distress and functional impairment.

T F   7. The biopsychosocial perspective is a holistic orientation also known as the adlerian formulation.

T F   8. A treatment formulation outlines the goals or outcomes for therapy and represents a mutually agreed upon blueprint for therapy.

Multiple Choice Questions

1. Which type of case formulation offers an explanatory statement and a rationale for the development of a clients functioning?

    a. Diagnostic
    b. Clinical
    c. Treatment
    d. A and B

2. Which case formulation(s) typically incorporates a specific theoretical background?

    a. Diagnostic
    b. Explanatory
    c. Clinical
    d. Both b and c

3. A client who fails to attend therapy sessions, shows up late for sessions, or "forgets" to do homework assignments is usually

    a. a client who is being treated without approval from third party payment providers.
    b. a client whose case formulation differs greatly from his or her therapist's formulation.
    c. a client with a DSM-IV diagnosed personality disorder.

4. Personality disorders fall under which axis on the DSM-IV diagnostic system?

    a. Axis I
    b. Axis II
    c. Axis III
    d. Axis IV

5. Major life stressors such as the occurrence of a recent divorce would fall under which axis on the DSM-IV diagnostic system?

    a. Axis I
    b. Axis II
    c. Axis III
    d. Axis IV

6. On which axis would a therapist note a diagnosis of bipolar disorder?

a. Axis I
b. Axis II
c. Axis III
d. Axis IV

7. A clinical formulation that is understood by looking at lifestyle patterns and family constellations is the

a. psychodynamic formulation.
b. cognitive-behavioral formulation.
c. adlerian formulation.
d. social formulation.

8. Which type of case formulation views symptoms as the manifestation of an individual's attempt to cope with life stressors?

a. Cognitive-behavioral formulation
b. Social formulation
c. Integrative formulation
d. Adlerian formulation

6

Focused and Ongoing Assessment

Learning Objectives

■ *A brief discussion of focused and ongoing assessment as it relates to "treatment outcomes research" and definitions of basic terms.*

■ *An overview of the treatment process from beginning to end, including a description of the "natural course of a psychological disorder" and the "recovery process" facilitated by psychotherapy.*

■ *Three types of symptoms and six areas of life functioning/functional impairment.*

■ *The skills of focused and ongoing assessment.*

■ *Application of focused assessment and ongoing assessment in an illustrated psychotherapy case.*

Chapter Outline

I.   Managed Care, Treatment Outcomes, and Assessment
   A. Definition of terms
II. The Treatment Process: From Beginning to End
   A. The natural course of a psychological disorder
   B. The course of clinical treatment and the recovery process
III. Focused Assessment
   A. Symptomatic manifestations
   B. Symptom types
   C. Types and levels of life functioning: six dimensions
      1. Self-management
      2. Intimacy
      3. Family
      4. Health

5. Work

6. Social

IV. Ongoing Assessment

Key Concepts

1. There are certain terms that apply to treatment outcomes and their assessment. Clinical outcomes describe the type and degree of symptoms or symptomatic distress. Functional outcomes describe the type and degree of client functioning. Treatment outcomes measurement is the quantification of clinical and functional outcomes during a specific period of time. Treatment outcomes monitoring is the periodic monitoring of treatment outcomes over time to assess overall impact of psychotherapy for the purpose of optimizing decisions regarding the course of treatment. Treatment outcomes management involves monitoring information to increase effectiveness of therapeutic services.

2. There tends to be a natural and predictable course of a psychological disorder. Treatment is beneficial in terms of lessening the duration and severity of a given disorder.

3. A typical trajectory involves a decline in life functioning with the occurrence of mild symptoms and distress. During this time individuals cope as best as they can. This is followed by demoralization. Coping resources are strained and functioning further declines. Next, as individuals continue to experience failure in their ability to cope, they move into a "sick role" and seek professional help.

4. This process is altered during the course of clinical treatment. Following the call for help, treatment initiates a healing sequence described as remoralization, remediation, and rehabilitation. When this sequence is effective, the predictable successful course of treatment is referred to as A-Tracking. When progress is not being made and there has been little or no clinical change noted in terms of symptom reduction, this is referred to as B-Tracking. Finally, when during the course of treatment symptomatic distress actually increases and functioning decreases, this is referred to as C-Tracking.

5. In focused assessment, the therapist notes both symptomatic manifestations and symptom types. Manifestations can be understood through three channels—biological, cognitive, and behavioral. Symptoms are complex and have different origins. The three symptom types are acute symptoms, persistent symptoms, and warning symptoms.

6. There are six areas of life functioning that should be examined to better understand a client. These areas include self-management, intimacy, family, health, work, and social. Each of these areas reflects a particular dimension in terms of the Biopsychosocial Model.

7. Ongoing assessment includes continuous monitoring of a client's mental status, health status, client resources, functional status, and treatment progress.

Learning Exercises

Refer back to and reread the case illustration of Mark detailed in Chapter 6 of this manual.

Exercise 1: Symptomatic Manifestations and Symptom Types

A. Manifestations refer to the biological, cognitive, and behavioral channels through which symptoms are expressed. Symptom types describe the intensity, quality, and timing of the symptoms.

1. Consider Mark's depressive symptoms. Which symptoms would you consider to be biological manifestations?

_____

_____

_____

2. Which symptoms are cognitive manifestations?

_____

_____

_____

3. Which symptoms are behavioral manifestations?

_____

_____

_____

B. Define the following symptom types and discuss the extent to which Mark's symptoms fit each symptom type.

1. Acute symptoms:

_____

_____

_____

2. Persistent symptoms:

_____

_____

_____

_____

3. Warning symptoms:

_____

_____

_____

_____

Exercise 2: Dimensions of Life Functioning

   1. Describe the dimension of self-management.

_____

_____

_____

   a. Address Mark's level of functioning in regards to self-management.

_____

_____

_____

_____

   b. How would you rate Mark's level of functioning in this area on a 1 to 10 scale where 1 is lowest or worst and 10 is highest or best?

_____

_____

   2. Describe the intimacy dimension of life functioning.

_____

_____

_____

   a. Address Mark's level of functioning in regards to intimacy.

_____

_____

_____

_____

b. How would you rate Mark's level of functioning in this area on a 1 to 10 scale where 1 is lowest or worst and 10 is highest or best?

_____

_____

3. Describe the family dimension of life functioning.

_____

_____

_____

a. Address Mark's level of functioning in regards to his family.

_____

_____

_____

_____

b. How would you rate Mark's level of functioning in this area on a 1 to 10 scale where 1 is lowest or worst and 10 is highest or best?

_____

_____

4. Describe the health dimension of life functioning.

_____

_____

_____

a. Address Mark's level of functioning in regards to his health.

_____

_____

_____

_____

    b. How would you rate Mark's level of functioning in this area on a 1 to 10 scale where 1 is lowest or worst and 10 is highest or best?

_____

_____

    5. Describe the work dimension of life functioning.

_____

_____

_____

    a. Address Mark's level of functioning in regards to work.

_____

_____

_____

    b. How would you rate Mark's level of functioning in this area on a 1 to 10 scale where 1 is lowest or worst and 10 is highest or best?

_____

_____

    6. Describe the social dimension of life functioning.

_____

_____

_____

    a. Address Mark's level of functioning in regards to social life.

_____

_____

_____

_____

b. How would you rate Mark's level of functioning in this area on a 1 to 10 scale where 1 is lowest or worst and 10 is highest or best?

_____

_____

Video Exercises

A. Watch the following video segment as Len Sperry works with Kathleen and demonstrates assessment of symptomatic distress.

1. What did you notice about these segments? What are your initial impressions?
2. How does Sperry elicit the client's understanding of what triggers her symptoms?
3. How is this information useful to the therapist?
4. How does Sperry discover this client's symptomatic manifestations?
5. What biological manifestations does this client experience?
6. What cognitive manifestations does this client experience?
7. What behavioral manifestations does this client experience?
8. Describe the intensity of this client's symptoms.
9. How does this information contribute to the therapist's development of a focused assessment?

Chapter Quiz

True and False Questions

T F   1. One example of a treatment goal that is accepted by most MBHOs is "individuation."

T F   2. Clinical outcomes are quantifications of the degree of symptoms or symptomatic distress that a client is experiencing.

T F   3. The duration and severity of psychological disorders are always lessened by psychotherapy.

T F   4. Kenneth Howard's Phase Theory Model involves a healing sequence of remoralization, remediation, and rehabilitation.

T F   5. While there is some variation between individuals, most clients experience the same symptomatic manifestations and triggers.

T F   6. Acute symptoms refer to mild symptomatic distress that causes impairment in one to three areas of life functioning.

T F   7. During ongoing assessment, the therapist continually evaluates mental, health, and functional status in addition to client resources and treatment progress.

T F   8. One way to monitor a client's progress of mental status is through administration of rating scales or self-reports.

Multiple Choice Questions

1. Which of the following do MBHOs typically view as appropriate goals for psychotherapy?

a. Symptom reduction
b. Restoration of functioning
c. Self actualization
d. Both a and b

2. Which term is defined as the use of outcomes monitoring information to increase overall treatment effectiveness and efficiency?

a. Clinical Outcomes
b. Treatment Outcomes Monitoring
c. Treatment Outcomes Management
d. Treatment Outcomes Measurement

3. A treatment outcome that describes a client's performance in his or her work environment is called

a. Clinical Outcome.
b. Functional Outcome.
c. Treatment Outcome.
d. Assessment Outcome.

4. Which trajectory track illustrates a decrease in overall functioning following clinical intervention?

a. A-tracking
b. B-tracking
c. C-tracking
d. None of the above

5. Which symptom type(s) might a cancer patient experience throughout the duration of their illness?

a. Acute symptoms
b. Persistent symptoms
c. Warning symptoms
d. Both a and b
e. All of the above

6. Which of the following statements are accurate?

a. Functional status refers to current or actual level of life functioning.
b. Functional capacity is assessed through self-reports.
c. Functional status refers to a client's potential level of functioning.
d. All of the above.

7. Which area is not considered one of the six dimensions of life functioning?

a. Self-management
b. Intrapersonal care
c. Family life
d. Social life

8. Which dimensions of life functioning are considered aspects of psychological functioning?

a. Self-management
b. Intimacy
c. Family
d. Both a and b
e. All of the above

9. Which dimensions are considered an aspect of social functioning?

a. Family
b. Work
c. Social

d. Both a and c

e. All of the above

10. Which dimensions of life functioning are considered an aspect of biological functioning?

a. Intimacy

b. Family

c. Health

d. Both a and c

e. All of the above

7

Intervention Strategies I

Learning Objectives

▪ *The role of cognitive and behavioral interventions in counseling.*

▪ *What cognitive restructuring is and how and when to use it.*

▪ *Important behavioral interventions including:*

a. *Desensitization, exposure, and relaxation skills*

b. *Social skills training skills*

c. *Modeling and behavioral rehearsal*

Chapter Outline

I.   Cognitive and Behavioral Interventions: Overview
II. Cognitive Restructuring
III. Automatic Thinking Patterns
    A. Meichenbaum's five ways to identify clients automatic thinking patterns
        1. Ask directly
        2. Imagery reconstruction
        3. Advice giving
        4. Self-monitoring
        5. Processing thoughts and behavior
    B. Four steps to happiness
        1. Identify the upsetting situation
        2. Help clients identify their negative feelings
        3. Use the triple column technique
        4. Have the client identify how much they believe in each of the automatic thoughts between zero and one hundred
IV. Desensitization, Exposure, and Relaxation Skills
    A. Systematic desensitization
    B. Eye movement desensitization and reprocessing

V. Social Skills Training
     A. Assertiveness training
     B. Problem-solving training
     C. Communication skill training
     D. Modeling and behavioral rehearsal

Key Concepts

1. Cognitive interventions seek to identify and change thought patterns that are based in irrational or faulty logic. Behavioral interventions are based on the idea that all behavior is learned behavior and can therefore be changed by unlearning or new learning.

2. Cognitive restructuring helps clients become aware of their automatic thinking patterns, change the way they process information and behavior, and change their beliefs about self, others, and the world.

3. Meichenbaum (1994) identified five ways to help clients become aware of their faulty beliefs and automatic thought patterns. These strategies include: asking directly; asking clients to relive or remember an event (imagery reconstruction); asking the client to give their own thoughts, feelings, and behaviors to problem situations (self-monitoring); and helping clients become aware of how they process information (processing thoughts and behaviors).

4. Burns (1999) has identified "four steps of happiness" that can be incorporated into a daily mood log to help clients identify automatic thought patterns and unhealthy beliefs. These include: (1) identifying the upsetting situation; (2) helping clients identify or label their negative feelings; (3) using the triple column technique to help clients identify automatic thoughts, identify the distortions in each faulty thought, and substitute more rational thoughts; and (4) have clients rate how much they believe in each automatic thought.

5. Systematic desensitization is a procedure that involves exposing an individual to an anxiety-provoking situation in a safe and relaxed state. A new approach to desensitization is known as eye movement desensitization and reprocessing (EMDR). This popular approach is used to help individuals deal with traumatic memories and claims to remove phobias in three sessions or less.

6. Social skills training is based on the following assumptions: interpersonal behaviors are based on a set of skills that are learned behaviors; social skills are situation specific; and effective use of social skills requires reinforcement. Social skills training programs include assertiveness training, problem-solving training, communication skill training, and modeling and behavioral rehearsal.

Learning Exercises

Exercise 1: Understanding Your Own Automatic Thoughts

1. Make a list of your beliefs and values.

_____

_____

_____

_____

_____

2. Which of those beliefs do you consider to be faulty or self-defeating? Why?

_____

_____

_____

_____

3. Choose one belief that you consider to be problematic and would like to change. Explain why.

_____

_____

_____

_____

4. Rate how much you believe in that problematic belief with 1 as lowest and 10 as highest.

_____

_____

5. How do you think this belief affects your feelings?

_____

_____

_____

_____

6. How do you think this belief might affect your behavior?

_____

_____

_____

_____

Exercise 2: Changing Automatic Thought Patterns

1. Complete the following: (a) write your negative thoughts and estimate your belief in each one (0–100), (b) identify the distortions in each automatic thought, (c) substitute more realistic thoughts and estimate your belief in each one.

Automatic Thoughts	Distortions	Rational Responses

Exercise 3: Behavioral Steps to Relaxation

The following is a relaxation exercise used to reduce daily tension and stress. This activity should be done on your own, in a quiet environment, free from distractions. The purpose of the activity is to systematically go through each muscle group, first tensing and then releasing and relaxing. Breathing is also used to unwind and quiet the mind. Before attempting this activity, read through the sequenced steps so that you are familiar with the exercise and need only refer to the guide periodically. During this activity, therapists often suggest that clients imagine themselves in a peaceful and comfortable place. Imagery is then used to enhance relaxation.

1. Begin by lying down on your back with your arms at your side and your eyes closed. Take slow deep breaths. You should inhale and exhale fully. Hold each breath after you've inhaled for approximately three to five seconds. Each time you exhale, allow yourself to relax further as you release the breath. Do this for several breathing cycles. You will continue the breathing pattern throughout the remainder of the exercises. Between each muscle group pause for two breathing cycles as you notice the difference between tense and relaxed muscles.

2. As you inhale deeply, make a tight fist with your hands. Hold the breath (three to five seconds) as you squeeze your fists tightly. Slowly release the tension in your hands as you exhale the breath.

(Pause for two breathing cycles)

3. As you inhale deeply, tighten your biceps. Hold the breath as you squeeze your biceps tightly. Slowly release the tension in your biceps as you exhale the breath.

(Pause for two breathing cycles)

4. As you inhale deeply, cross your arms over your chest and squeeze your shoulders. Hold the breath as you squeeze your upper body tightly. Slowly release the tension in your arms and shoulders as you exhale the breath.

(Pause for two breathing cycles)

5. As you inhale deeply, tighten your stomach muscles. Hold the breath as you squeeze your abdomen tightly. Slowly release the tension in your stomach muscles as you exhale the breath.

(Pause for two breathing cycles)

6. As you inhale deeply, tighten your buttocks. Hold the breath as you squeeze your buttocks tightly. Slowly release the tension in your buttocks as you exhale the breath.

(Pause for two breathing cycles)

7. As you inhale deeply, tighten your thighs. Hold the breath as you squeeze your thighs tightly. Slowly release the tension in your thighs as you exhale the breath.

(Pause for two breathing cycles)

8. As you inhale deeply, tighten your calf muscles by flexing your foot. Hold the breath as you squeeze your calf muscles tightly. Slowly release the tension in your calf muscles as you exhale the breath.

(Pause for two breathing cycles)

9. As you inhale deeply, point your toes. Hold the breath as you squeeze your toes tightly. Slowly release the tension in your toes as you exhale the breath.

(Pause for two breathing cycles)

10. As you inhale deeply, tighten your biceps. Hold the breath as you squeeze your biceps tightly. Slowly release the tension in your toes as you exhale the breath.

(Pause for two breathing cycles)

11. As you inhale deeply, tense the muscles of your upper forehead. Hold the breath as you squeeze the muscles tightly. Slowly release the tension in your upper forehead as you exhale the breath.

(Pause for two breathing cycles)

12. As you inhale deeply, squeeze your eyes shut tightly. Hold the breath as you squeeze the muscle group tightly. Slowly release the tension in your eyes as you exhale the breath.

(Pause for two breathing cycles)

13. As you inhale deeply, tighten your jaw by biting your teeth together. Hold the breath as you squeeze your jaw tightly. Slowly release the tension in your jaw as you exhale the breath.

Video Exercises

A. Watch the following video segment as Richard Stuart works with Wesley and Adel.

1. What did you notice about this segment? What are your initial impressions?
2. What is the negative belief that this client holds about herself?
3. How does the therapist identify this belief?
4. Do you think the client believes that this belief is distorted?
5. How might a therapist help this client work with this belief?

B. Watch the following video segment as Richard Stuart explains how Wesley's words or behaviors trigger Adel's distorted thinking patterns.

1. What did you notice in this video segment? What are your initial reactions?
2. How do Adel's automatic thoughts affect her relationship with Wesley?
3. How do automatic thoughts interfere with how individuals process information?

C. Watch the following video segment as Richard Stuart shares a personal example of how behaviors can affect feelings.

1. What did you notice in this segment? What are your initial reactions?
2. What is Stuart suggesting in this segment?
3. What is the relationship between feelings, thoughts, and behaviors?

D. Watch the following segment as Richard Stuart explains the concept of "acting as if."

1. What did you notice in this video segment? What are your initial reactions?
2. Explain the concept of "acting as if."
3. How does this concept apply to the use of cognitive-behavioral interventions?

E. Social skills training methods are employed by therapists to help clients learn the necessary skills to improve their functioning. Watch the following video segment as Gus Napier demonstrates modeling of assertive behavior.

1. What did you notice about this segment? What are your initial reactions?
2. How does Napier demonstrate modeling?
3. How does Napier demonstrate the use of assertiveness?
4. Why is this social skill so important for this client?

Chapter Quiz

True and False Questions

T F   1. Cognitive-behavioral therapists believe that cognitions can be identified and modified.

T F   2. Schemas are core beliefs through which individuals process information and behavior.

T F   3. Negative thought patterns decrease available coping skills and can lead to disorders such as depression and anxiety.

T F   4. Automatic thoughts are usually conscious patterns that are readily identified by the client.

T F   5. Relaxation is the first and most important step in any desensitization procedure.

T F   6. During the process of systematic desensitization it is best to begin with an anxiety provoking situation that is highest on the client hierarchy.

T F   7. Culture has little impact on social skills training curriculum.

T F   8. Goal clarification is an essential component of assertiveness training.

T F   9. Problems such as interpersonal difficulties and phobias respond well to behavioral rehearsal and modeling.

T F   10. Modeling and behavioral rehearsal is effective for learning new ways to think and feel.

Multiple Choice Questions

1. What is the primary goal of cognitive restructuring?

a. For individuals to recognize faulty thinking

b. For individuals to adopt new and more effective beliefs

c. For individuals to change the way they process information and behavior

d. All of the above

2. Overgeneralization is a form of distorted thinking. Which statement best describes this type of thinking?

a. No matter how much you achieve you still feel worthless.

b. You assume people's reactions to you are negative without any evidence that this is true.

c. You failed once so you assume that you will always fail.

d. All of the above.

3. Which form of distorted thinking fits the following statement: "I have the worst luck. I just know this will turn out badly."?

a. Magnification or minimization

b. Jumping to conclusions

c. Personalization and blame

d. Emotional reasoning

4. One method of understanding the role that thoughts play in behavior is

a. A-B-C of emotion

b. Systematic desensitization

c. Cognitive expression

d. Both a and c

5. Which method for identifying faulty beliefs in clients involves asking a client to remember and review a significant event?

a. Self-Monitoring

b. Processing thoughts and behavior

c. Imagery reconstruction

d. None of the above

6. Which method for identifying faulty beliefs in clients might involve an examination of the metaphor of prejudice?

a. Imagery reconstruction
b. Advice giving
c. Self-monitoring
d. Processing thoughts and behaviors

7. The Triple-Column Technique includes an examination of

a. Automatic thoughts
b. Cognitive distortions
c. Alternative responses
d. All of the above

8. What technique is used to help clients deal with stress and anxiety?

a. Systematic desensitization
b. Relaxation
c. Eye movement desensitization and reprocessing
d. All of the above

9. Which forms of training focuses on helping clients clarify their goals or intentions?

a. Social Skills Training
b. Assertiveness Training
c. Problem-Solving Training
d. Modeling and Behavioral Rehearsal

10. Which form of training focuses on observing and imitating effective behavior?

a. Social Skills Training
b. Assertiveness Training
c. Communication Training
d. Modeling and Behavioral Rehearsal

8
Psychodynamic Interventions

Learning Objectives

- *The role of psychodynamic interventions in counseling.*
- *The definition of insight and the role insight plays in counseling.*
- *Interpretation in counseling and how counselors gain interpretation skills.*
- *Intervention skills that contribute to clarification and insight including:*
  - *a. summarizing*
  - *b. clarifying meaning*
  - *c. establishing connections*
  - *d. challenging discrepancies, incongruencies, and destructive behavior*
  - *e. exploring transference and counter transference*

Chapter Outline

I.   Psychodynamic Interventions: Overview
II. Psychodynamic Interviewing Skills: Utility and Value
    A. Summarizing
    B. Encouraging clients to elaborate
    C. Clarifying
        1. Deletions
        2. Distortions
        3. Generalizations
    D. Making connections
III. Therapeutic Confrontation Skills
    A. Confronting body language

B. Confronting immediate behavior

C. Confronting destructive behaviors

IV. Interpretation Skills in Counseling

A. Guidelines for interpretation

B. Levels of interpretation

C. Dealing with transference and counter transference

Key Concepts

1. Therapists use psychodynamic interventions to address fears, intentions, and defenses that individuals are not consciously aware of, but which influence people's thoughts, feelings, attitudes, and behaviors. These interventions are learned skills that are often viewed as challenging by clients, but the skills help clients understand the beliefs that underlie their behavior.

2. Therapists summarize a client's story by gathering and organizing key pieces of the client's message and presenting this information to the client to check for understanding and to keep the client on track. Therapists also use summarizations to make suggestions about the client's message of which the client may not be consciously aware. The therapist is then able to offer the client a potentially accurate, but somewhat different perspective.

3. Therapists use open-ended verbalizations and gentle commands to encourage clients to elaborate on their emotions, thoughts, or behaviors. The focus of these questions, verbalizations, and gentle commands is always client centered, such that the client is encouraged to elaborate on what he or she is doing, thinking, and feeling. Questions that begin with "how" or "what" or commands that begin with "Help me understand . . ." are effective in eliciting client talk and encouraging clients to link emotions to thoughts and behaviors.

4. Therapists often find it necessary to clarify a client's message. By carefully attending to the client, therapists will notice deletions, distortions, and generalizations. A deletion is when important information is left out of the client's story. A distortion is a representation of a process as fixed or closed. The client presents an ongoing process as "closed," suggesting that he or she has no control over the outcome. Generalizations are phrases that shift a perspective from specific to universal.

5. Therapists help clients make connections between their thoughts, feelings, and behaviors. Establishing connections helps break down a client's interactions such that clients discover the relationship between specific triggers and responses. This helps clients become aware of and change unproductive patterns.

6. Therapeutic confrontational skills are used to bring the client's attention to inconsistencies in his or her story. Therapists confront clients about discrepancies between verbal and nonverbal messages, immediate in-session behaviors, and destructive behaviors.

7. Interventions made by therapists are most effective when following these guidelines: a client-therapist relationship should be established before attempting interpretive interventions; therapists should allow clients to discover their own insight whenever possible; and therapists should be aware of their clients reactions to their interpretations.

8. Transference refers to the feelings that the client has toward the counselor based on the client's previous relationships. Counter transference refers to the

feelings that the client brings forth in the counselor, which are related to the counselor's own relationships. Therapists deal with transference and counter transference through immediacy. Immediacy involves the counselor responding to something as it occurs in the session, in other words, the focus is on the here and now.

Learning Exercises

Exercise 1: Generating Effective Summarizations, Encouraging Clients, and Making Connections

A. Betty, a 35-year-old marketing executive, is discussing a difficult day at work. "Today was a terrible day at the office. I gave a presentation of a new marketing plan that I'd been working on for two weeks. My boss ripped it apart. He knows how much work I put into developing this plan and he didn't seem to appreciate any of it. He humiliated me and this wasn't the first time he's done it. I was so steamed. I just walked right out of the conference room. He makes me feel like an incompetent child."

Write an appropriate summarization for this client.

_____

_____

_____

_____

Write two possible open-ended verbalizations for this client using the provided prompts.

(1) How . . .

_____

_____

_____

(2) What . . .

_____

_____

_____

Write three effective gentle commands for this client using the provided prompts.

(1) Help me understand . . .

_____

_____

_____

(2) I'm not sure I understand . . .

_____

_____

_____

(3) I'm wondering about . . .

_____

_____

_____

B. Betty continues her story.

"By 5:00 I was out the door, but traffic was horrendous. You can imagine how crazy sitting in traffic makes me after a long day at the office. Anyway, I was so happy to get home, but when I walked in the door, the house was a mess and the boys were just sitting there watching TV. I nearly blew my top. I really let them have it. After all, don't they realize I'm working all day? The least they can do is have the house clean when I get home. I don't know. Maybe I was too harsh on them . . ."

Write an appropriate summarization for this client.

_____

_____

_____

_____

Write two possible open-ended verbalizations for this client using the provided prompts.

(1) How . . .

_____

_____

_____

(2) What . . .

_____

_____

_____

Write three effective gentle commands for this client using the provided prompts.

(4) Help me understand . . .

_____

_____

_____

(5) I'm not sure I understand . . .

_____

_____

_____

(6) I'm wondering about . . .

_____

_____

_____

Exercise 2: Making Connections Between Thoughts, Feelings, and Behaviors. Continuing Your Work with Betty.

Refer to part A of exercise 1:

1. What was Betty doing when her day became "a terrible day at the office"?

_____

_____

2. What might Betty have been thinking?

_____

_____

3. What was Betty feeling?

_____

_____

4. How would you help Betty connect and better understand her thoughts, feelings, and behaviors?

_____

_____

_____

Refer to part B of exercise 1:

1. What did Betty do when she returned from the office?

_____

_____

_____

2. What might Betty have been thinking when she got home?

_____

_____

_____

3. What was Betty feeling?

_____

_____

_____

4. How would you help Betty connect and better understand her thoughts, feelings, and behaviors?

_____

_____

_____

Exercise 2: Clarifying Deletions, Distortions, and Generalizations—Helping Clients Be More Specific

1. A woman, 21 years old, is talking about her unplanned pregnancy. "I don't even talk to the father anymore. He hates me. It's not like I tried to get pregnant. I don't know what I'll do. I'll never be able to afford this baby on my own."

Identify the deletion in this client's message.

_____

_____

Identify the distortion in this client's message.

_____

_____

Identify the generalization in this client's message.

_____

_____

How might you respond to this client to help her clarify the missing or deleted information?

_____

_____

_____

How might you respond to this client to help her clarify the distortion in her message?

_____

_____

_____

How might you respond to this client to help her clarify the generalization in her message?

_____

_____

_____

2. A man, 38 years old, is talking about his desire to change careers. "I've been in construction for over twenty years now. Sometimes I don't think I could do anything else. I never did go to college. I'm considering a career change, but well, you know, transitions never go smoothly."

Identify the deletion in this client's message.

_____

_____

Identify the distortion in this client's message.

_____

_____

Identify the generalization in this client's message.

_____

_____

How might you respond to this client to help him clarify the missing or deleted information?

_____

_____

_____

How might you respond to this client to help him clarify the distortion in his message?

_____

_____

_____

How might you respond to this client to help him clarify the generalization in his message?

_____

_____

_____

3. A woman, 29, is talking about her failure to quit smoking. "I've tried everything out there. You name it, I've tried it. I just couldn't quit. I think it is stress related. I'm always stressed out. How is a person supposed to quit smoking when they are always so stressed? I guess I have more pressing issues to worry about than quitting smoking."

Identify the deletion in this client's message.

_____

_____

Identify the distortion in this client's message.

_____

_____

Identify the generalization in this client's message.

_____

_____

How might you respond to this client to help her clarify the missing or deleted information?

_____

_____

_____

How might you respond to this client to help her clarify the distortion in her message?

_____

_____

_____

How might you respond to this client to help her clarify the generalization in her message?

_____

_____

_____

4. A young lady, 16 years old, is talking about dropping out of school. "My parents are freaking out. But why should I care about high school? No one there cares about me. I never was a good student anyway."

Identify the deletion in this client's message.

_____

_____

Identify the distortion in this client's message.

_____

_____

Identify the generalization in this client's message.

_____

_____

How might you respond to this client to help her clarify the missing or deleted information?

_____

_____

_____

How might you respond to this client to help her clarify the distortion in her message?

_____

_____

_____

How might you respond to this client to help her clarify the generalization in her message?

_____

_____

_____

Video Exercises

A. Watch the following video segment as James Bitter demonstrates the use of open-ended verbalizations and gentle commands.
1. What did you notice about this segment? What are your initial reactions?
2. How did Bitter use a gentle command? What did he say?
3. How effective was this technique?
4. Why would Bitter want to know about the family's typical day? How is that information helpful to the therapist?

B. Watch the following video segment as O'Hanlon demonstrates the use of clarifying skills.
1. What did you notice about this segment? What are your initial reactions?
2. How did O'Hanlon clarify Adrian's and Judy's assumption that Pam never does anything on her own?
3. What information did the family "leave out"?
4. Why is this information important?
5. How effective is this technique?

C. Watch the following video segment as Insoo Kim Berg demonstrates confronting discrepancies, and incongruencies.

1. What did you notice about this segment? What are your initial reactions?
2. How did Berg demonstrate confronting skills?
3. What incongruence do you think Berg picked up on?
4. How do you think the client may have been inconsistent?
5. How effective is this technique?

D. Watch the following video segment as Ken Hardy demonstrates the use of therapeutic confrontational skills.

1. What did you notice about this segment? What are your initial reactions?
2. What specific confrontational skills did Hardy demonstrate?
3. How did Hardy confront a discrepancy occurring in Phil's life?
4. Why do you think this technique is useful?

E. Watch the following video segment as Hardy continues to work with Phil and establishes connections between his thoughts and behaviors.

1. What did you notice about this segment? What are your initial reactions?
2. How effectively did Hardy establish connections between Phil's thoughts, behaviors, and the results he experiences?
3. How do you think this technique impacted Phil?
4. Why do you think this technique is useful?

Chapter Quiz

True and False Questions

T F   1. Psychodynamic interventions are often thought of as quick fixes for client problems.

T F   2. If a client gains insight into life patterns, change will occur.

T F   3. Providing a holding environment is helpful when using some challenging psychodynamic interventions.

T F   4. Summarizations allow therapists to slightly change the meaning or focus of a client's message so that the message is more client-centered.

T F   5. Gentle commands offer direction to the client but do not limit the client.

T F   6. A distortion is when the client lies or presents a deliberate untruth in the therapy session.

T F   7. One way a therapist confronts a client is by noticing and commenting on body language.

T F   8. A therapist should always confront destructive behaviors to self or others.

T F   9. Interpretations should be given firmly to ensure that the client will accept the therapists point of view.

T F   10. Immediacy is a positive way of responding to transference and counter transference.

Multiple Choice Questions

1. Which statement does not describe psychodynamic interventions?

a. Psychodynamic interventions address clients' anxieties, fears, motives, and defense mechanisms.

b. Psychodynamic interventions help clients gain insight so that they can better understand themselves.

c. Psychodynamic interventions focus on thoughts, feelings, and behaviors.

d. None of the above.

2. How does change occur when using psychodynamic interventions?

a. Change depends on insight, without insight change cannot occur.

b. Change occurs when therapists inform clients of insights.

c. Change occurs when clients have an understanding and are willing to act on that understanding.

d. All of the above.

3. Which statement best describes summarizing?

a. Summarizing focuses on retelling the client's story.

b. Summarizing focuses on significant issues and conveys meaning.

c. Summarizing focuses on deletions, distortions, and generalizations.

d. All of the above

4. Which statement(s) best describes open-ended verbalizations and gentle commands?

a. Open-ended verbalizations and gentle commands encourage clients to elaborate on emotions, thoughts, and behaviors.

b. Open-ended verbalizations are questions that typically begin with words such as "How" or "What."

c. Gentle commands are statements that give a client some direction.

d. All of the above

5. When a client leaves out important parts of his or her story, the client is using

a. deletions.

b. distortions.

c. generalizations.

d. all of the above.

6. "I really hate myself for not losing weight." This statement is an example of a

a. deletion.

b. distortion.

c. generalization.

d. Both b and c.

7. Helping clients link certain situations with specific responses such as "When you . . ., then you . . ." is called

a. clarifying.

b. making connections.

c. encouragement.

d. generalizations.

8. Which statement is most accurate regarding the use of confrontation?

a. Confrontation skills should not be used with clients of different cultures because they require a cultural understanding of nonverbal behaviors.

b. Confrontations regarding discrepancies between verbal and nonverbal communications should be sensitive to differences in culture.

c. Therapists should check out their impressions regarding discrepancies with all clients before making assumptions.

d. Both b and c.

9. Therapists' intuitions are based on

a. cultural background.
b. training or education.
c. life experiences.
d. all of the above.

10. When a therapist discovers a feeling of resentment toward a client who reminds the therapist of her ex-husband, the therapist is experiencing

a. transference.
b. counter transference.
c. a moral dilemma.
d. both a and b.

9

Interventive Interviewing and Solution-Focused Interventions

Learning Objectives

- *What interventive interviewing is and how it originated.*

- *The significant impact that interventive interviewing can have on the therapy process.*

- *A description of ten key interventive interviewing questions—including "scaling" questions, which are probably the most often used intervention of this type.*

- *How and when to use these interventions.*

- *How interventive interviewing links individual and couples/family therapy.*

Chapter Outline

I. Therapeutic and Interventive Interviewing: An Overview
   A. Origins of interventive interviewing
   B. Interventive interviewing/questioning skills: their clinical use and value
      1. Diagnostic-linear questions
   C. How clinician's intentionality determines question types
II. Ten Types of Interventive Interviewing Questions
   A. Circular questions
   B. Reflective questions
   C. Strategic questions
   D. Externalizing questions
   E. Empowering questions

   F. Scaling questions

   G. Exception questions

   H. Positive description questions

   I. Outcome questions coping questions

  III. How and When to Use Interventive Questioning: A "Map" For Doing Therapy

   A. The initial interview

   B. In subsequent sessions

Key Concepts

1. The distinction between diagnostic interviewing and therapeutic interviewing is blurred due to concerns about cost containment. Interventive interviewing is one form of therapeutic interviewing that focuses on provoking change. Alfred Adler first talked about this form of interviewing in general terms. However, the concept was not fully developed and named until Karl Tomm brought it to the forefront of therapeutic theory. Since then the idea has been modified and refined by therapists such as Tomm, White, Epston, Berg, de Shazer, and Miller.

2. Circular questions help the therapist elicit the type and extent of relational patterns that connect people. The clinician's intention is to prompt the client to reframe the situation in a new and more positive way.

3. Reflective questions help clients view a situation in a different frame of reference by considering alternative perspectives. The clinician's intention is to prompt the client to use his or her own resources to solve problems.

4. Strategic questions focus on altering an individual's behavior or correcting dysfunction. The clinician's intention is to indirectly confront the client's resistance to change.

5. Externalizing questions help the client to experience a problem as external or separate from the self. The clinician's intention is to reduce hopelessness and facilitate belief in change.

6. Empowering questions help clients recognize their strengths, knowledge, and experience that can be useful in solving problems. The clinician's intention is to increase self-efficacy.

7. Scaling questions ask clients to rate their experience on a continuum. The clinician's intention is to better assess the client's perception of symptomatic distress and impairment.

8. Exception questions highlight times when the client's problems or symptoms do not occur. The clinician's intention is to assess whether those times and circumstances can serve as a model for successful change. The therapist helps the client notice past successes, which encourages clients to work toward future success.

9. Positive description questions help to reframe a client's negatively stated goals to more positive, achievable goals. The clinician's intention is to open the possibility for clients to be free to experience their unique sense of self.

10. Outcome questions help therapists elicit and understand the client's goals for therapy or endpoint for change. The clinician's intention is to help clients clarify and specify their expectations for treatment outcomes.

11. Coping questions indirectly reframe clients' experience in terms of their capacity to cope with difficult circumstances or external influences. The clinician's intention is to assist the client to explore times in which he or she has used successful coping skills.

12. It is essential that therapists tailor their questioning strategies to fit the situational demand of the client.

Learning Exercises

Exercise 1: Choosing and Formulating Effective Client Questions

A. A woman, 37, is fighting cancer. "Mostly, I'm concerned about how my illness is impacting my children. I'm always so tired after my treatments. I just feel as if I am failing as a mother. I don't have the energy to listen to them. I don't have the patience that I once had. All I have is this illness and it is tearing me down. Sometimes I think they are on autopilot. I mean, they were both doing so well in school. But now Johnny is acting out. His teacher had to call me the other day. I feel like it is my fault. I know I'm not giving him enough attention at home."

1. What is a possible effective coping question?

_____

_____

Why is this an effective question for this particular client?

_____

_____

_____

2. Choose a second possible coping question.

_____

_____

Why is this an effective question for this particular client?

_____

_____

_____

3. What is a possible effective empowering question?

_____

_____

Why is this an effective question for this particular client?

_____

_____

_____

4. Choose a second possible empowering question.

_____

_____

Why is this an effective question for this particular client?

_____

_____

_____

5. What is a possible effective positive description question?

_____

_____

Why is this an effective question for this particular client?

_____

_____

_____

6. Choose a second possible positive description question.

_____

_____

Why is this an effective question for this particular client?

_____

_____

_____

7. What other types of questions might be effective in helping this client? Choose two questions, label the question type, and explain your clinical intention in using each of them.

Question 1:

_____

_____

Your Clinical Intention:

_____

_____

_____

Question 2:

_____

_____

Your Clinical Intention:

_____

_____

_____

B. A man, 29 years old: "We were only married for a year and she just left. It happened two years ago now but I still can't handle it. I just feel so depressed. I started dating about six months ago. It was going ok for a while with one lady, but then I just messed things up. I don't know what happened. I guess I started talking about the divorce and it must have scared her away. I don't know. It just isn't worth dating anymore. I feel like I'll end up getting hurt again. I'm tired of feeling so depressed."

1. What is a possible effective externalizing question?

_____

_____

Why is this an effective question for this particular client?

_____

_____

_____

2. Choose a second possible externalizing question.

_____

_____

Why is this an effective question for this particular client?

_____

_____

_____

3. What is a possible effective exception question?

_____

_____

Why is this an effective question for this particular client?

_____

_____

_____

4. Choose a second possible exception question.

_____

_____

Why is this an effective question for this particular client?

_____

_____

_____

5. What is a possible effective scaling question?

_____

_____

Why is this an effective question for this particular client?

_____

_____

_____

6. Choose a second possible scaling question.

_____

_____

Why is this an effective question for this particular client?

_____

_____

7. What other types of questions might be effective in helping this client? Choose two questions, label the question type, and explain your clinical intention in using each of them.

Question 1:

_____

_____

Your Clinical Intention:

_____

_____

_____

Question 2:

_____

_____

Your Clinical Intention:

_____

_____

_____

C. A woman, 45 years old, is overweight. "I've tried for years to lose the weight. I've never been able to do it. I'm tired of trying. I know what the health risks are. But you know what? I just don't care anymore. I don't care what I look like. I don't even care what I feel like. I don't want to try another diet that I'm just going to fail. Sometime I wonder why I even bother coming to therapy."

1. What is a possible effective strategic question?

_____

_____

Why is this an effective question for this particular client?

_____

_____

_____

2. Choose a second possible strategic question.

_____

_____

Why is this an effective question for this particular client?

_____

_____

_____

3. What is a possible effective outcome question?

_____

_____

Why is this an effective question for this particular client?

_____

_____

_____

4. Choose a second possible outcome question.

_____

_____

Why is this an effective question for this particular client?

_____

_____

_____

5. What other types of questions might be effective in helping this client? Choose two questions, label the question type, and explain your clinical intention in using each of them.

Question 1:

_____

_____

Your Clinical Intention:

_____

_____

_____

Question 2:

_____

_____

Your Clinical Intention:

_____

_____

_____

D. A woman, married for 13 years. "My husband is always working. I know that they have been putting a lot of stress on him at the office, but I'm starting to feel like we are just second best. It's been a sore subject at home lately. He's always late for dinner and by the time he gets home, I'm already so aggravated. It just ends up being a big mess. I start to wonder where his priorities are."

1. What is a possible effective circular question?

_____

_____

Why is this an effective question for this particular client?

_____

_____

_____

2. Choose a second possible circular question.

_____

_____

Why is this an effective question for this particular client?

_____

_____

_____

3. What is a possible reflective question?

_____

_____

Why is this an effective question for this particular client?

_____

_____

_____

4. Choose a second possible reflective question.

_____

_____

Why is this an effective question for this particular client?

_____

_____

_____

5. What other types of questions might be effective in helping this client? Choose two questions, label the question type, and explain your clinical intention in using each of them.

Question 1:

_____

_____

Your Clinical Intention:

_____

_____

_____

Question 2:

_____

_____

Your Clinical Intention:

_____

_____

_____

Exercise 2: Practicing Your Skills

Meet with your learning partner. You will each take turns acting as the therapist and the client. Each of you should use an audiotape to record your session. Refer to the text section titled, "How and When To Use Interventive Questioning: A Map For Doing Therapy." This section details the start of a first interview with a client. As the client, talk about a time when you felt pressure or stress in your life. As the therapist, focus on gathering data, assessing the level of distress, and assessing client outcome expectancies. Feel free to jot down a few notes. Continue with the session for fifteen to eighteen minutes. Then switch roles. After you have both completed your exercises, take a few minutes to reflect and listen to your tape.

1. What did you learn about the client, as a person?

_____

_____

_____

2. What did you learn about the client's symptoms?

_____

_____

_____

3. How would you characterize the client's level of impairment?

_____

_____

_____

4. What are the client's expected outcomes for therapy?

_____

_____

_____

5. How effectively did you use initial interviewing questions?

_____

_____

_____

6. Where would you go from here?

_____

_____

_____

Video Exercises

A. Watch the following video segment as Frank Pittman demonstrates the use of circular questioning.
1. What do you notice about how Pittman phrases the question?
2. What do you notice about how the client responds to the question either verbally or nonverbally?
3. How effective do you think this question was in this particular segment?
4. Under what circumstances could you imagine yourself using this technique?

B. Watch the video segment as Insoo Kim Berg demonstrates the use of reflective questioning.
1. What do you notice about how Insoo Kim Berg phrases the question?
2. What do you notice about how the client responds to the question either verbally or nonverbally?
3. How effective do you think this question was in this particular segment?
4. Under what circumstances could you imagine yourself using this technique?

C. Watch the video segment as Jon Carlson demonstrates the use of strategic questioning.
1. What do you notice about how Carlson phrases the question?
2. What do you notice about how the client responds to the question either verbally or nonverbally?
3. How effective do you think this question was in this particular segment?
4. Under what circumstances could you imagine yourself using this technique?

D. Watch the video segment as Steve Madigan demonstrates the use of externalizing questions.
1. What do you notice about how Madigan phrases the question?
2. What do you notice about how the client responds to the question either verbally or nonverbally?
3. How effective do you think this question was in this particular segment?
4. Under what circumstances could you imagine yourself using this technique?

E. Watch the video segment as Jon Carlson demonstrates the use of empowering questions.

1. What do you notice about how Carlson phrases the question?
2. What do you notice about how the client responds to the question either verbally or nonverbally?
3. How effective do you think this question was in this particular segment?
4. Under what circumstances could you imagine yourself using this technique?

F. Watch the video segment as Jon Carlson demonstrates the use of scaling questions.

1. What do you notice about how Carlson phrases the question?
2. What do you notice about how the client responds to the question either verbally or nonverbally?
3. How effective do you think this question was in this particular segment?
4. Under what circumstances could you imagine yourself using this technique?

G. Watch the video segment as Bill O'Hanlon demonstrates the use of exception questions.

1. What do you notice about how O'Hanlon phrases the question?
2. What do you notice about how the client responds to the question either verbally or nonverbally?
3. How effective do you think this question was in this particular segment?
4. Under what circumstances could you imagine yourself using this technique?

H. Watch the video segment as Steve Madigan demonstrates the use of positive description questions.

1. What do you notice about how Madigan phrases the questions?
2. What do you notice about how the client responds to the questions either verbally or nonverbally?
3. How effective do you think these questions were in this particular segment?
4. Under what circumstances could you imagine yourself using this technique?

I. Watch the video segment as Insoo Kim Berg demonstrates the use of outcome questions.

1. What do you notice about how Insoo Kim Berg phrases the question?
2. What do you notice about how the client responds to the question either verbally or nonverbally?
3. How effective do you think this question was in this particular segment?
4. Under what circumstances could you imagine yourself using this technique?

J. Watch the video segment as Cheryl Rampage demonstrates the use of coping questions.

1. What do you notice about how Rampage phrases the question?
2. What do you notice about how the client responds to the question either verbally or nonverbally?
3. How effective do you think this question was in this particular segment?
4. Under what circumstances could you imagine yourself using this technique?

Chapter Quiz

True and False Questions

T   F   1. Alfred Adler first described the ideas behind the concept of interventive interviewing.

T   F   2. The primary focus of interventive interviewing is to provoke change in early therapy sessions and throughout subsequent sessions.

T   F   3. Therapists can utilize interventive interviewing questions in the very first therapy session.

T   F   4. Interventive interviewing questions are used in individual, couple, and family therapy.

T   F   5. Diagnostic linear questions are similar to interventive interviewing questions except diagnostic linear questions are more focused on facilitating change.

T   F   6. The same question, under varying contexts, can be seen as diagnostic-linear, circular, and reflective.

T   F   7. Reflective questions, like circular questions, are based on a circular pattern.

T   F   8. The main purpose of empowering questions is to separate one's self from the presenting problem.

T   F   9. One advantage of scaling questions is that they give responsibility for change back to the client.

T   F   10. When a client is feeling ambivalent about change, it is helpful to use externalizing questions.

Multiple Choice Questions

1. Why are interventive questioning skills useful?
   a. Diagnostic questions are no longer being used in therapy.
   b. Change and movement can occur during the very first therapy session.
   c. Interventive interviewing makes the therapy process more client-focused.
   d. Both b and c.

2. Which statement is most accurate?
   a. Interventive interviewing questions should be used instead of diagnostic-linear questions.
   b. Interventive interviewing questions are more useful than diagnostic-linear questions.
   c. Interventive interviewing questions and diagnostic-linear questions have different functions and should be used together.
   d. None of the above.

3. Which type of interventive interviewing question seeks to provide a corrective influence on the client?
   a. Circular questions
   b. Strategic questions
   c. Externalizing questions
   d. Reflective questions

4. Which type of interventive interviewing question seeks to elevate hopelessness by encouraging clients to see problems as separate from their selfhood?
   a. Circular questions

    b. Strategic questions
    c. Externalizing questions
    d. Exception questions

5. Which type of interventive interviewing questions demonstrates how event (A) can influence event (B) at the same time that event (B) influences event (A)?

    a. Circular questions
    b. Outcome questions
    c. Externalizing questions
    d. Exception questions

6. The so called "miracle question" by de Shazer is an example of which type of interventive interviewing question?

    a. Positive description questions
    b. Outcome questions
    c. Externalizing questions
    d. Coping questions

7. The goal of eliciting a client's sense of self-efficacy is the main component in

    a. empowering questions.
    b. outcome questions.
    c. positive description questions.
    d. strategic questions.

8. "What will you be doing instead of feeling depressed and dejected?" This is an example of a(n)

    a. empowering question.
    b. outcome question.
    c. externalizing question.
    d. positive description question.

9. It is best to use strategic questions when

    a. clients appear discouraged and helpless.
    b. clients would benefit from gaining insight.
    c. clients appear stuck or resistant.
    d. all of the above.

10. It is best to use circular and reflective questions when

    a. clients appear discouraged and helpless.
    b. clients would benefit from gaining insight.
    c. clients appear stuck or resistant.
    d. all of the above.

10

Intervention Strategies IV: Systemic and Psycho-Educational Interventions

Learning Objectives

▪ *Understand how structural techniques can change systems.*

▪ *How to use systemic and structural techniques to create disequilibrium.*

▪ *How to create different perceptions of reality as a precursor to change.*

▪ *How to create different behavior through psycho-education and pattern interruption.*

Chapter Outline

I. Overview
   A. "Place Psychology" affects and is affected by:
      1. Cultural, ethnic, racial, geographic, and other socioeconomic factors
      2. The individual's birth order position within the family
      3. The sense of loyalty to the family and the degree of individuation and differentiation among the members
      4. The distribution of power and how decisions are made
      5. The roles within the system
      6. The alliances and collusions among the members and the triangulation that interferes with dyadic relationships
      7. The degree of physical or emotional closeness and distance among members
   B. Structural strategies can be used to:

1. Create movement
2. Change perspectives
3. Shift distribution of power
4. Disrupt coalitions
5. Form new alliances
6. Clarify boundaries between and among subsystems
7. Discover new aspects of selves
8. Normalize the experience of being in a particular place
9. Reframe the meaning of being in a particular place
10. Change the family system while working with one individual

II. Techniques for Disequilibrium
   A. Creating a different sequence of events
      1. Enactment
      2. Boundary marking
   B. Creating different perceptions of reality
      1. Reframing
      2. Re-labeling
      3. Punctuation
      4. Unbalancing
      5. Boundary restructuring
      6. Paradoxes
   C. Creating different behavior
      1. Teaching communication
      2. Learning to resolve conflict and negotiate problems
      3. Choices and problem solving
      4. Assigning tasks

Key Concepts

1. Therapists can use specific interventions designed to intentionally challenge and unbalance a family system, which is understood as the core social context through which lasting change can occur. These interventions increase stress on the family system and open the door for structural change.

2. Place psychology, conceptualized by Alfred Adler and coined by Sherman and Dinkmeyer, emphasizes how clients subjectively perceive their place in the family system and the world, and how their behavior is related to that perception.

3. A new therapeutic system is created when the therapist intervenes with the family. Structural techniques serve as a guide for the therapist in this process. The therapist joins with the family without being absorbed into their system. This process is often called joining, rapport, accommodating, or transference. Structural strategies are meant to bring about change by reorganizing the family system.

4. Structural strategies may be used for the following purposes: to create movement, change perspectives, shift the distribution of power, disrupt coalitions, form new alliances, clarify boundaries between and among the subsystems, discover new aspects of selves, normalize the experience of being in a

particular place, reframe the meaning of being in a particular place, and to change the family system while working with one individual.

5. Therapists promote change by creating a different sequence of events. This is often done through enactment. Enactment is a technique that allows the therapist to observe problematic behavioral sequences within the family system and a vehicle through which the therapist disrupts the family's transactional patterns. The therapist temporarily assumes control of the rules that regulate who should interact with whom, about what, when, and for how long. By changing these interactional patterns, the therapist helps family members change their perceptions of the problem. One case of enactment is boundary marking, whereby the therapist defines areas of interaction either verbally or physically.

6. Therapists seek to create different perceptions of reality through reframing, re-labeling, re-punctuation, unbalancing, boundary restructuring, and paradoxical techniques. Reframing is a strategy that gives new meaning to or changes the perspective of the presenting problem. Re-labeling involves substituting a positive adjective for the negative ones used in the placing of blame on one family member from another. Punctuation is a term referring to a pattern of behavior in which each individual family member attributes the problem to the other. A therapist re-punctuates the situation to prevent the redundant communication patterns. Unbalancing is when a therapist uses his or her authority to break a stalemate by supporting one of the family members in the conflict. Boundary restructuring is a technique the therapist uses to realign relational boundaries by either increasing closeness or distance. Therapists use paradoxical interventions to prompt family members to search for alternatives to their current situations.

7. Therapists also work to create different behaviors in family systems by breaking up patterns that support the problems. Since effective communication and problem solving skills are considered essential for a functioning family system, teaching clients to communicate, to negotiate for problem resolution, and to make choices is a core aspect of therapy. Therapists also assign tasks or homework to help clients accomplish the goals of therapy.

Learning Exercises

Exercise 1: Birth Order and Your Family Structure

1. What was your childhood like for you?

_____

_____

_____

_____

_____

2. How would you describe yourself as a child?

_____

_____

_____

_____

3. What was school like for you?

_____

_____

_____

_____

4. How would you describe yourself as a student?

_____

_____

_____

_____

5. Describe your peer group.

_____

_____

_____

_____

6. What was your role in relation to your peer group?

_____

_____

_____

_____

7. Make a list of yourself and your siblings in order from oldest to youngest. Write a short description of each individual on your list.

_____

_____

_____

8. Which sibling is most like you? How?

_____

_____

_____

9. Which sibling is most different from you? How?

_____

_____

_____

10. Were any alliances formed among your siblings? What about alliances between individual siblings and either or both of your parents? Explain.

_____

_____

_____

_____

_____

11. How did you and each of your siblings relate to your mother?

_____

_____

_____

_____

12. How did you and each of your siblings relate to your father?

_____

_____

_____

_____

13. What role do you think you played in relation to your siblings?

_____

_____

_____

_____

14. What role do you think you played in relation to your parents?

_____

_____

_____

_____

15. How do you think you found your place in your family of origin?

_____

_____

_____

_____

16. How has your role in relation to your siblings changed since you were a child?

_____

_____

_____

_____

17. How has your role in relation to your parents changed since you were a child?

_____

_____

_____

_____

Exercise 2: Understanding Perspective

1. Think about a recent problem that occurred between you and another member of your family. Describe the circumstances of that problem.

_____

_____

_____

_____

_____

2. What is your perception of why the problem occurred?

_____

_____

_____

_____

3. What might be your family member's perception of why the problem occurred?

_____

_____

_____

_____

_____

4. How might an objective third party (perhaps a therapist) reframe this situation so that it could be acceptable to both you and your family member?

_____

_____

_____

5. How does the idea of punctuation apply for you and your family member in this particular problem?

_____

_____

_____

_____

Exercise 3: Understanding Boundaries

1. What types of boundaries exist in your family system?

_____

_____

_____

2. Would you consider these boundaries to be rigid or diffuse? Explain.

_____

_____

_____

3. How do these boundaries affect your relationship with your family members?

_____

_____

_____

_____

4. How do these boundaries affect your family's functioning?

_____

_____

_____

_____

Exercise 4: Learning to Communicate

1. How well do you think you communicate with your siblings?

_____

_____

_____

_____

2. How well do you communicate with your mother?

_____

_____

_____

_____

3. How well do you communicate with your father?

_____

_____

_____

_____

4. What could you do to communicate more effectively with your family members?

_____

_____

_____

_____

5. How could increased or more effective communication better your family's problem solving skills?

_____

_____

_____

_____

Video Exercises

A. Structural family therapists focus on helping families develop boundaries and appropriate hierarchies. Watch the following video segment as Harry Aponte demonstrates this in his work with Judy (mother) and Pam (daughter).

1. What did you notice about this segment? What are your initial reactions?
2. How does this segment demonstrate the use of structural interventions?
3. What specific structural techniques did you notice Aponte use in this segment?
4. What are some of the suggestions Aponte offers to Judy?
5. How might those suggestions lead to the development of stronger boundaries/hierarchies?

B. During the video session, Aponte discovers a strong alliance between Pam and her father, Adrian, but notices a great deal of tension between Pam and Judy. Watch as Aponte works with this family using structural interventions.

1. What did you notice about this segment? What are your initial reactions?
2. How and why does Aponte attempt to restructure this particular family dynamic?
3. How does this segment demonstrate the use of structural interventions?
4. What specific structural techniques did you notice Aponte use in this segment?
5. Discuss the interplay of alliances, hierarchies, and subsystems.

C. Watch the following video segments as Philip Guerin demonstrates the use of structural interventions with Pam, Judy, and Adrian.

1. What did you notice about these segments? What are your initial reactions?
2. What does Guerin notice about the relationship between Pam, Judy, and Adrian?
3. How would you characterize the relationships in this family based on these segments?
4. What specific techniques does Guerin use to work with this family?

D. START: "What would happen if you won a lottery and part of it was that you won a condo . . . START: "So everybody ought to just leave you alone with it."

5. What did you notice about this segment? What are your initial reactions?
6. What does Guerin notice about the relationship between Pam, Judy, and Adrian?
7. How would you characterize the relationships in this family based on this segment?
8. What specific techniques does Guerin use to work with this family?

Chapter Quiz

True and False Questions

T F   1. Structural strategies are used to create organizational change in the family system and between family members.

T F   2. Sherman and Dinkmeyer first conceptualized the ideas behind "place psychology."

T F   3. An individual's birth order impacts his or her role in the family system.

T F   4. Therapists seek to disturb the family system by creating dysfunction.

T F   5. Through enactment, the therapist assumes control over the rules that govern communication between family members.

T F   6. One method a therapist uses to mark boundaries is blocking interaction patterns among members of a system.

T F   7. Most family problems can be broken down and explained by a linear model of cause and effect.

T F   8. A therapist might align with one family member over another to create unbalance.

T F   9. Modeling is an effective way to teach communication skills.

T F   10. When brainstorming solutions to problems, only accept ideas that will likely produce change.

Multiple Choice Questions

1. An individual's place or role in a family system is affected by

a. cultural, ethnic, racial, geographic, and other socioeconomic factors.
b. the individual's birth order position within the family.
c. the individual that initiated therapy.
d. both a and b.

2. A major assumption for the use of structural strategies is

a. all behaviors have purpose and meaning.
b. it is the therapist's role to define the family's system.
c. each individual family member serves a useful function in the family system.
d. both a and c.
e. both a and b.

3. Structural strategies can be used to

a. disturb family systems.
b. create family dysfunction.
c. form new alliances.
d. both a and b.

4. When one family member assumes a new role in the family system

a. the system collapses.
b. therapy is concluded.
c. change occurs.
d. all of the above.

5. A strategy used to shed new light or offer new perspective on a problem is called

a. re-labeling.
b. re-mixing.
c. reframing.
d. restructuring.

6. When a therapist tells the family that they are not capable of doing anything different than what they are currently doing, the therapist is

a. restraining.
b. relabeling.
c. redefining.
d. prescribing.

7. Therapists can unbalance a family system by

a. aligning with a family member who has less power.
b. refusing to recognize a family member.
c. preventing the disengaged family members from avoiding one another.
d. all of the above.

8. Which of the following is an example of the use of paradox?

a. Asking family members to resolve problems.
b. Encouraging clients to postpone decisions, thus prolonging a crisis situation.
c. Assigning tasks or homework to family members.
d. None of the above.

9. Which of the following is not an important consideration in choice making?

a. Clearly secure your desired outcomes before making a choice.
b. Identify what you want to accomplish.
c. Be aware of how your choices influence others.
d. None of the above.

10. Which is not a suggested technique, according to the text, for getting clients to follow through on assignment completion?

a. Examine the negative consequences of not resolving their problem.
b. Reward the client with positive reinforcement for completing the task.
c. Talk about everything the client has done to try to solve the problem.
d. Use your authority as a therapist to get the client to follow through.

11
Maintaining Clinical Gains, Preventing Relapse, and Terminating Treatment

Learning Objectives

- *Strategies to maintain therapeutic change.*
- *What relapse prevention is and how to utilize it.*
- *How to effectively terminate and setup treatment follow-up.*

Chapter Outline

I. Treatment Adherence/Maintenance
   A. Treatment adherence guidelines
      1. Anticipate non-adherence
      2. Consider treatment from the client's perspective
      3. Facilitate a collaborative relationship that is based on negotiation
      4. Be client oriented (understand the clients' view/explanatory model)
      5. Tailor treatment
      6. Enlist family support
      7. Provide a system of continuity and accessibility
      8. Don't give up
II. What is Relapse Prevention (RP)?
   A. RP research and treatment characteristics
      1. Flexibility in treatment content
      2. Flexibility in treatment format
      3. Identifying and modifying salient behaviors
      4. Focusing on reasonably changeable behaviors
      5. Effectively generalizing from therapy to the client's world

    B. Why clients relapse

    C. Relapse prevention

    D. Change in treatment focus

    E. Open ended treatment

    F. Steps to RP

        1. Create a treatment alliance

        2. Tailor treatment

        3. Manage stress

        4. Increase positive interaction and encouragement

        5. Skill training

III. Termination

    A. Types of termination

        1. Suggested termination

        2. Imposed termination

        3. Situational termination

        4. Early termination

    B. Methods and process of termination

IV. Chapter summary

Key Concepts

1. The following guidelines have been established for therapists to maximize treatment adherence. Therapists need to think about adherence at the beginning of treatment and should actually anticipate non-adherence. Therapists should consider treatment from the client's perspective. A collaborative relationship that is based on negotiation should be established between therapist and client. Therapists should focus on understanding the client's views and explanatory model. Therapists should consider, adjust, and modify treatment to fit the needs of each individual client. It is useful for therapists to enlist family support. Therapists should provide a system of continuity and accessibility to the therapy process and should never give up on that process.

2. Relapse prevention (RP) is a psycho-educational program that is designed to teach clients who are trying to change their behavior how to anticipate and cope with the problem of relapse. This program was initially based on the principles of social-learning theory and combines behavioral skill training procedures and cognitive intervention techniques with systems thinking. Relapse is often thought of as both a process and an outcome. However, viewing it as a process implies that there are choices that can be made and interventions that can be applied by both the therapist and the client to make changes.

3. Relapse prevention has received a considerable amount of research. The following treatment characteristics emerged as a result of that research. First, treatment must be carefully tailored to each client. Second, the treatment format and structure, such as length and spacing of sessions needs to remain flexible. Third, therapists must gather a full picture of the client's functioning by identifying and modifying salient behaviors. Fourth, it is important to focus on reasonably changeable behaviors. Fifth, therapists must design interventions that can be effectively generalized from therapy to the client's world.

4. Relapse occurs because of human nature. The combination of high-risk situations, little or no coping skills, and negative expectancies increase the likelihood that relapse will occur. These factors can be mitigated by helping clients gain self-control, thereby developing feelings of confidence in their ability to handle and solve problems. Clients can then replace negative expectancies with positive ones that can serve as obtainable goals.

5. Treatment should not only seek to reduce negative behaviors—it should focus on identification and creation of positive experiences and behaviors. This change in focus enables clients to learn to define progress based on realistic goals. Intervention techniques should be aimed at both initial behavior change and maintenance of the changed behavior.

6. The following five steps have been established to facilitate relapse prevention. First, therapists must engage the client to create a treatment alliance. Second, therapists must tailor treatment to match the individual client's needs. Third, treatment should focus on stress management. Fourth, in order to maintain positive relationships, clients should be taught to increase positive interactions and encouragement. Fifth, therapists must teach effective skills and design appropriate interventions that facilitate generalization from the context of treatment to daily life.

7. Therapists should discuss the notion of termination with clients at the beginning of therapy with an open-ended viewpoint. Clients should be encouraged to return to therapy whenever the need arises. The therapist should consider the impact of termination on the client, the client's history of separations, the likelihood that the client will regress, and the client's perception of termination before determining how termination will be approached. Most approaches to termination involve gradual tapering off of sessions, therapeutic vacations, or direct termination.

Learning Exercises

Exercise 1: Defining Relapse Prevention (RP) and Understanding RP Research

1. How is the concept of relapse prevention defined?

_____

_____

_____

_____

_____

2. Why is it important to view relapse prevention as a process?

_____

_____

_____

_____

_____

3. Why is flexibility in treatment content and treatment format important in preventing relapse?

_____

_____

_____

_____

4. Why is it important to monitor overt, emotional, and cognitive behaviors in clients?

_____

_____

_____

_____

5. How can therapists help clients to focus on specific changeable behaviors?

_____

_____

_____

_____

_____

6. What steps can be taken to help improve generalization of treatment?

_____

_____

_____

_____

_____

Exercise 2: The Five Steps to Facilitate Relapse Prevention

1. How can therapists work to create a treatment alliance?

_____

_____

_____

_____

_____

2. Why is it important for therapists to tailor treatment?

_____

_____

_____

_____

_____

3. How can therapists tailor treatment?

_____

_____

_____

_____

_____

4. Can you think of two examples of different treatment interventions for different clients' needs?

_____

_____

_____

_____

_____

5. How can therapists teach clients to manage stress?

_____

_____

_____

_____

_____

6. How does a client's sense of self-efficacy impact the likelihood of relapse?

_____

_____

_____

_____

_____

7. What other factors influence the likelihood of relapse?

_____

_____

_____

_____

_____

8. How can therapists help to mitigate these factors?

_____

_____

_____

_____

_____

9. What are the benefits of teaching clients encouragement skills?

_____

_____

_____

_____

_____

10. How could a therapist teach encouragement skills?

_____

_____

_____

_____

_____

11. How would a therapist use skill training to help clients generalize treatment to daily life?

_____

_____

_____

_____

_____

Exercise 3: Understanding the Methods and Process of Termination

1. Describe the four types of termination.

_____

_____

_____

_____

_____

2. As a therapist in training, how comfortable are you with the process of termination?

_____

_____

_____

_____

3. How will you discuss termination with your clients?

_____

_____

_____

_____

4. How do you feel about therapy as a life long process?

_____

_____

_____

_____

5. Under what circumstances might further treatment no longer be in the client's best interests?

_____

_____

_____

_____

_____

Video Exercises

A. Watch the following video segments as G. Alan Marlatt works with Danny to develop a therapeutic alliance.

1. What did you notice about these video segments? What are your initial reactions?
2. What questions does Marlatt ask to help him understand this particular client's perspective?
3. What does Marlatt discover about this client's personal resources?
4. What does Marlatt discover about this client's motivation for change?
5. What does Marlatt discover about this client's barriers to treatment?
6. How does this information help a therapist in tailoring a treatment program?
7. How does this information help a therapist in anticipating non-adherence?

B. Watch the following video segment as Marlatt continues to work with Danny.

1. What did you notice about this video segment? What are your initial reactions?
2. What technique does Marlatt use to elicit an understanding of the client's acceptance of responsibility?
3. How can this understanding help a therapist work with a client to prevent relapse?

Chaper Quiz

True and False Questions

T F   1. Therapists can prevent or minimize relapses by anticipating non-adherence and working to curtail its occurrence.

T F   2. Understanding the client's explanatory model is not a key component of relapse prevention.

T F   3. The therapist and client should discuss potential barriers to treatment.

T F   4. Relapse prevention programs are based on principles of social learning theory.

T F   5. Non-adherence occurs with ninety percent of all clients seeking treatment.

T F   6. Research shows that tailored treatments help secure benefits of therapy.

T F   7. Relapse occurs because many clients lack the willpower to successfully complete a treatment program.

T F   8. A person's sense of self-efficacy influences his or her treatment outcomes.

T F   9. In order to maintain a satisfying relationship, individuals should strive to maintain a ratio of five positive interactions to one negative interaction.

T F   10. The therapist should be the only one to terminate therapy.

Multiple Choice Questions

1. Which is not an example of a suggested technique for enhancing treatment adherence?

a. Therapists should tailor their treatment plan.
b. Therapists should focus on the individual rather than the system.
c. Therapists should simplify treatment directives.
d. Therapists should use role-play and paradoxical techniques.

2. The therapist should assess

a. the client's beliefs and misconceptions about his or her problem.
b. the client's goals for therapy.
c. the client's sense of self-efficacy.
d. all of the above.

3. Relapse is defined as

a. a return of a problem behavior following a problem-free period.
b. a process and an outcome.
c. the same a lapse in behavior.
d. both a and b.
e. all of the above.

4. What were the results of Whisman's research regarding the effectiveness of booster sessions?

a. Booster sessions significantly minimized occurrences of relapse.
b. Booster sessions do not impact relapse prevention.
c. Booster sessions may be beneficial but require further research.
d. All of the above.

5. Relapse occurs with most individuals because

a. people lack willpower.
b. people have weak character.
c. people need total control to succeed.
d. both a and c.
e. none of the above.

6. Adler and Bandura might agree that

a. past success often leads to future success.
b. if an individual has not experienced past successes he or she will not expect to encounter future successes.
c. the client's expectation that relapse will occur seems to be a powerful predictor of relapse.
d. all of the above.

7. A major aspect of relapse prevention is

a. identification of high-risk situations.

b. use of self-monitoring and self-efficacy ratings.

c. holding treatment sessions at the client's home or office to facilitate generalization.

d. both a and b.

e. all of the above.

8. Following a lapse in behavior, the therapist should typically

a. increase the number of treatment interventions.

b. administer negative reinforcement.

c. both a and b.

d. all of the above.

e. none of the above.

9. Termination that is initiated by the therapist signifies that the client has made significant progress and is, from the therapists perspective, close to the goals of treatment, is called

a. suggested termination.

b. imposed termination.

c. situational termination.

d. early termination.

10. Termination that occurs because the therapist feels that further treatment is not in the client's best interest is known as

a. suggested termination.

b. imposed termination.

c. situational termination.

d. early termination.

12

Practical Issues and Ethical Dilemmas

Learning Objectives

- *A suggested protocol for handling initial contact, intake, and a first session with a new client.*

- *Legal and ethical issues that frequently arise in counseling practice.*

- *Managing boundaries inside and outside the session.*

- *Effective use of supervision, consultation, and referral resources.*

- *Using the Internet as a resource for counseling.*

Chapter Outline

Key Concepts

1. Both beginning and experienced therapists encounter ethical issues. The fields of counseling and psychology have specific codes of ethics or professional conduct. These codes are available online with both the American Counseling Association and the American Psychological Association. Involvement in professional publications, organizations, Internet based information services, and development opportunities help therapists stay abreast to specific ethical and practical issues.

2. It is essential that therapist consider pre-counseling contact with clients. Interactions with the public should be conducted in a conscientious and ethical manner, as should any marketing efforts on behalf of a therapist or agency. Therapists must represent themselves and their services appropriately.

3. Initial contact, intake, and the first session with a client are each essential factors in the outcome of therapy. Clients need to know about the counseling process and what to expect in counseling. Clients should be provided information regarding the extent to which their privacy and confidentiality will be maintained; the expected number and frequency of therapy sessions; what to do in case of an emergency; financial arrangements including fees, methods of payment, and insurance coverage; how a missed appointment, cancellation, or late arrival for an appointment will be handled; their right to withdraw from counseling; their right to request a different therapist; the training, experience, and theoretical approach of the therapist; the nature of supervision and/or consultation the therapist would receive; and the potential benefits and risks of therapy.

4. Basic information should be exchanged and certain goals should be met in the initial assessment. These goals include: establishing a sound engagement of the patient in a therapeutic alliance; to collect a valid data base; to develop an evolving and compassionate understanding of the patient; to develop an assessment from which a tentative diagnosis can be made; to develop an appropriate disposition and treatment plan; and to affect some decrease of anxiety in the patient.

5. Boundaries must be established both within and outside of therapy. Ethical considerations regarding boundaries and dual relationships should be held in the highest regard. Therapists should look to training and supervision to support their efforts in the treatment process and ensure therapeutic benefits to their clients. Therapists should periodically assess their clients' perceptions of progress in therapy. Therapists may choose to ask clients to evaluate the extent to which the particular session met their needs.

6. The advent of the Internet offers many conveniences to both the therapist and the client. However, the following factors should be considered to help you to evaluate the usefulness of that information: the authority or credibility of the information provided; the purported purpose of the site; the objectivity of the materials presented; the currency of information provided; how useful the information provided is in meeting you or your client's needs; and how easy it is to obtain information from the site.

Learning Exercises

Exercise 1: Understanding Ethical and Practical Issues

A. Refer to the text regarding Sam, the counselor in private practice, who was hired to teach a class in counseling therapy at the local university as a substitute for a professor who became ill. Recall that Sam announced to the class that he would offer a reduced rate to any clients students referred to him.

1. Why is this inappropriate?

_____

_____

_____

_____

2. How could Sam have ethically increased his clientele for his private practice?

_____

_____

_____

_____

3. What if one of Sam's students requested that Sam be her counselor? How would he appropriately handle that situation?

_____

_____

_____

_____

4. Why would it be inappropriate for Sam to counsel one of his own students?

_____

_____

_____

_____

B. Refer to the text regarding Tom, who had an Ed.D. in school administration, and returned to school to get a masters degree in counseling. Recall that the agency staff referred to him as "Dr. Tom." This led his clients to believe that he had a doctorate degree in counseling or psychology.

1. Why is this inappropriate or unethical?

_____

_____

_____

_____

2. How might Tom have handled this differently to ensure proper understanding of his credentials?

_____

_____

_____

_____

C. Refer to the text regarding Mary, who had recently passed her state licensure exam, and decided to go into private practice. Recall that while Mary's training and experience prepared her for individual counseling, she decided to list herself in the "Yellow Pages" as a therapist specializing in "Marriage, Family, Child, and Individual Therapy."

1. Why is this inappropriate or unethical?

_____

_____

_____

_____

2. What type of training must a therapist receive in order to offer services in a particular area?

_____

_____

_____

_____

3. How could Mary have appropriately expanded her area of expertise?

_____

_____

_____

_____

Exercise 2: Informed Consent

Refer to information given in the text as well as information regarding informed consent given in the code of ethics for the American Psychological Association (APA), the American Counseling Association (ACA), or other professional organizations to which you belong. This information can be found online, as discussed in the text.

1. What issues should be discussed with your clients for informed consent?

_____

_____

_____

_____

2. Write an informed consent document that you might give to clients.

_____

_____

_____

_____

_____

_____

_____

_____

_____

_____

_____

_____

_____

_____

_____

3. How did you decide what information to include in this document?

_____

_____

_____

_____

4. How do you feel about discussing these issues with your clients?

_____

_____

_____

_____

5. Are there any particular issues that you would feel uncomfortable discussing?

_____

_____

_____

_____

6. Pair up with a partner in class and practice going over the information you chose to include in your informed consent document. What did your partner include that you did not?

_____

_____

_____

_____

7. What would you change about your informed consent document?

_____

_____

_____

_____

8. Would you cover all of the information during a first session?

_____

_____

_____

_____

Exercise 3: Practicing Initial Client Contact

Pair up with your learning partner. Each of you will take turns acting as the therapist and the client. It is recommended that you videotape your client initiation so that you may review this tape and evaluate your performance. Practice your greeting approach. As suggested in the text, consider seating arrangements, eye contact, auditory, verbal, nonverbal, and kinesthetic factors. Next, practice discussing with your client the information you provided in your informed consent document. This exercise should take approximately fifteen minutes for each partner to complete. After you have reviewed your tape, answer the following questions.

1. What did you notice as the client?

_____

_____

_____

_____

2. What did you feel like as the client?

_____

_____

_____

_____

3. What feedback would you give to your learning partner regarding the initial greeting?

_____

_____

_____

_____

4. What feedback would you give to your learning partner regarding discussion of informed consent issues?

_____

_____

_____

_____

5. What did you notice as the therapist?

_____

_____

_____

_____

6. How did you feel as the therapist?

_____

_____

_____

_____

7. What feedback would you give yourself regarding your initial greeting?

_____

_____

_____

_____

8. What feedback would you give yourself regarding your discussion of informed consent issues?

_____

_____

_____

_____

Video Exercises

A. It is essential to consider cultural factors when building therapeutic relationships. Watch the following video segments as Jon Carlson and Mary Arnold work with a couple and consider their cultural context in an initial therapy session.

1. What did you notice in this segment? What are your initial reactions?
2. How does understanding an individual's, couple's, or family's culture help the therapist to work more effectively?
3. How does the cultural backgrounds of the couple in the video influence their relationship?
4. Are there any common themes between Martha and John and their respective cultures?

B. Initial greetings vary among therapists. Some therapists choose to open an initial session by allowing the client to ask any questions they might have. Watch the following video segment as Lenore Walker begins an initial session with Gina.

1. What did you notice about this segment? What are your initial reactions?
2. How do you think Gina responded to Walker's initial comments?
3. How do you see yourself opening an initial therapeutic interview?

C. When concluding an initial interview the therapist often briefly summarizes what was covered in the therapy session or offers suggestions to the client. Watch the following video segments as Insoo Kim Berg and Arnold Lazarus demonstrate closing an initial therapy session.

1. What did you notice about these video segments? What are your initial reactions?
2. How do the clients seem to respond to Lazarus's summary and closing of the session?
3. How do the clients seem to respond to Berg's summary and closing of the session?
4. What suggestions does Lazarus offer to his client?
5. What suggestions does Berg offer to her client?
6. What is different and what is similar about Lazarus's and Berg's closings?

Chapter Quiz

True and False Questions

T   F   1. Counselors adhere to the ethical guidelines established by the American Psychological Association.

T   F   2. Ethical standards regarding confidentiality do not apply to web counseling due to the format through which counseling takes place.

T   F   3. It is appropriate for therapists to disclose their credentials and offered services to the public.

T F   4. A therapist may provide services to clients outside their range of formal training.

T F   5. Therapists should discuss methods of payment with clients up front or prior to the initiation of the therapeutic process.

T F   6. It is inappropriate for therapists to take notes during therapy sessions because note taking violates confidentiality.

T F   7. Clients should participate in the development of their treatment plan including goals, strategies, and treatment expectancies or outcomes.

T F   8. Supervision is a process inherent in the therapeutic process, therefore it is unnecessary to obtain the client's written consent.

T F   9. One aspect of learning to establish boundaries is learning to effectively close a session within the discussed amount of time.

T F   10. The Internet can be seen as a resource for counseling but web sites must be evaluated to determine credibility.

Multiple Choice Questions

1. Therapist can maintain and increase their knowledge of available resources by
   a. developing their own ethical rules based on experience.
   b. referring to the code of ethics established by their appropriate professional organization.
   c. both a and b.
   d. none of the above.

2. The three phases of counseling established by DePauw, which require ethical consideration, include
   a. initial phase, counseling phase, and termination phase.
   b. pre-counseling phase, service provision phase, and termination phase.
   c. pre-counseling phase, counseling phase, and termination phase.
   d. none of the above.

3. Which is considered an inappropriate method for recruiting potential clients?
   a. Putting an advertisement in the yellow pages.
   b. Taking referrals from social service agencies.
   c. Holding a community parenting class.
   d. Establishing a community workshop program.
   e. None of the above.

4. Informed content should be given to the client
   a. in written form.
   b. verbally.
   c. during the first session.
   d. all of the above.

5. Therapists must provide clients with
   a. the potential benefits and risks of therapy.
   b. their right to request a different therapist.
   c. the therapist's home phone number in case of emergency.
   d. both a and b.
   e. all of the above.

6. Basic information including a client's name, address, phone number, best times available, and method of payment should be established by

a. an intake worker.
b. the therapist.
c. either the intake worker or the therapist, or whomever has initial contact with the client.

7. At the end of a first session the therapist should have gathered enough information to

a. diagnose the client.
b. develop a treatment plan.
c. estimate the number of sessions to meet the client's goals.
d. both a and b.
e. both b and c.

8. How should a therapist deal with a client who consistently brings up "big issues" at the end of the allotted time for therapy?

a. Allow the client to continue beyond the scheduled time if the issue is significant.
b. Maintain firm boundaries regarding session time and schedule an intermediate session if necessary.
c. All of the above.

9. What factors should be considered before treatment is terminated?

a. The client's ability to maintain the gains made in therapy.
b. The client's attachment to the therapist.
c. How the change affects client's family members and other individuals in the client's world.
d. All of the above.
e. Both b and c.

10. When might treatment termination occur?

a. When the goals for counseling are met.
b. When the therapist and client have completed the agreed upon number of sessions.
c. When the client decides to terminate treatment for any number of reasons.
d. All of the above.

13

A Therapist's Diary: An "Obsessive" Client

After reading Chapter 13 and completing the exercises in the text, consider the following:

1. How does this therapist's work with Janet match your concept of what the process of psychotherapy looks like?

_____

_____

_____

_____

_____

2. To what extent does this case illustration conform or not conform to the way the media portrays psychotherapy?

_____

_____

_____

_____

3. What are your perceptions regarding the effectiveness of this approach to therapy?

_____

_____

_____

_____

4. If you were a consultant in this case, what might you have done differently?

_____

_____

_____

_____

_____

5. If you learned that this client was Jamaican American, how might this change your formulation and interventions?

_____

_____

_____

_____

_____

6. To what extent do you think culture impacts therapeutic relationships, case formulations, and interventions?

_____

_____

_____

_____

_____

7. Assume that an HMO would only provide for six sessions with this client. How would you tailor your treatment approach?

_____

_____

_____

_____

_____

Video Segments and Questions

Chapter 2

A. Clients often have their own explanatory model or explanation for why their symptoms are occurring. Clients also tend to have specific expectations for the outcome of treatment, their goals of treatment, and the occurrence of change in therapy. Furthermore, clients often have specific ideas about their role and the therapist's role in the therapeutic process. Watch the following video segments of Jill and David Scharff working with Judy, Pam, and Adrian.

START: "Well, thanks for coming in, Adrian, Pam, and Judy ..." END: "I can still talk but it would be repetitious of what I said last time."

1. What did you notice about this video segment? What are your initial reactions?
2. How do Adrian's (the father) comments define his role in this session?
3. How do Adrian's comments define his wife's (Judy) role in the session?
4. How does Adrian define his daughter's (Pam) role in the session?
5. How do you think this sets up the role of the therapist in this session?

START: Scharff: "Apparently they have some complaints, what do they complain about?" END: Judy: "And to answer us when we talk to her. She doesn't give you an answer."

1. What did you notice about this video segment? What are your initial reactions?
2. How does David Scharff elicit Pam's understanding of the family's problem?
3. What is Pam's explanation for the family's problem?
4. How does David Scharff elicit the clients' expectations or goals for therapy?
5. What does Judy suggest as the families goals for therapy?

B. Empathy is a key factor in achieving engagement. Therapists use empathetic responding to help clients feel truly heard and understood. Watch the following video segment of Jill and David Scharff working with Judy, Pam, and Adrian.

START: "Judy, when you go to the grave you want to be alone ..." STOP: "Things just weren't gelling together with the holidays."

1. What did you notice about this video segment? What are your initial reactions?
2. How effectively do you think Jill Scharff used empathy in responding to Judy?
3. Do you think Judy felt heard and understood?
4. Do you think Judy felt safe to talk about and experience the emotion she was feeling?

5. How does the use of empathy help to achieve engagement in therapy?
6. Do you think that Judy was engaged in the therapy session? Explain.

Chapter 3

A. Watch the following segment as James Bugental works with Gina and demonstrates the use of internal attending. Discuss this segment with your classmates by answering the following questions:

START: Gina: "I find it best when starting something like this to make a transition." STOP: "Yeah—inside I have to be perfect."

1. What did you notice about this video segment? What are your initial reactions?
2. How effective was the internal attending activity that Bugental used?
3. What information did Bugental learn about Gina by using this internal attending activity? How did the conversation following centering activity help Bugental to understand Gina?
4. Do you think you could use a centering activity similar to the one demonstrated here? Why or why not?

B. Watch the following segment as Bugental demonstrates the use of both attending and joining skills (internal, physical, and verbal attending) and active listening skills (minimal prompts, reflecting content, reflecting feeling, and silence). Discuss this segment with your classmates and answer the following questions:

START: Gina: "I like to fix things . . . my hunch is there must be a lot of hurt down there someplace and the mocking keeps the hurt down." END: ". . . because it's kind of fooling yourself when you laugh to hide the pain."

1. What did you notice in this segment? What are your initial reactions?
2. How did Bugental demonstrate the use of attending and joining skills? What specific skills could you identify in this video segment?
5. How did Bugental demonstrate active listening skills? What specific active listening skills could you identify in this video segment?
6. How do you think Gina felt during this segment?

C. Watch the following segment as Ken Hardy demonstrates the use of both attending and joining skills (internal, physical, and verbal attending) and active listening skills (minimal prompts, reflecting content, reflecting feeling, and silence). Discuss this segment with your classmates and answer the following questions:

START: "I was curious about your laugh." STOP: ". . . and I know that's not really healthy."

1. What did you notice in this segment? What are your initial reactions?
2. How effective was Hardy's use of attending and joining skills? What specific skills could you identify in this video segment?
3. How did Hardy demonstrate active listening skills? What specific active listening skills could you identify in this video segment?
4. How do you think Phil (the client) felt during this segment?

Chapter 4

A. Therapists begin the formal-diagnostic assessment by gaining an understanding of the client's presenting problem. Through this process, the therapist gains a great deal of information regarding the clients current functioning. Watch both Ken Hardy and Jon Carlson demonstrate the initiation of a diagnostic assessment.

(Hardy) START: "I'm sure since you were willing to come in . . . something you're struggling with . . . if you could just give me a sense of what that is . . ." STOP: "That's good. That's great."

1. What did you notice in this segment? What are your initial reactions?
2. What do you see as Phil's (the client) presenting problem?
3. What questions did Hardy ask to elicit this story from Phil?
4. What aspects of Phil's life did Hardy elicit in this segment?
5. How would you assess Phil's current functioning based on this segment?
6. What aspects of Phil's life would he like to improve?
7. How effective was this initial segment of a diagnostic assessment?

START: (start at very beginning of clip) END: "Yes, yes that's a big one."

1. What did you notice about this video segment? What are your initial reactions?
2. What do you see as Gina's (the client) presenting problem?
3. What questions did Carlson ask to elicit this story from Gina?
4. What aspects of Gina's life did Carlson elicit in this segment?
5. What components of the formal-diagnostic assessment could you apply to this segment?
6. What are your initial reactions to this segment?
7. How effective was this initial segment of a diagnostic assessment?

Chapter 5

A. Watch the following segment as Lazarus discusses his view of an appropriate treatment plan for Juan.

START: "So if we were going to move into a second session . . ." STOP: "I wouldn't mind that, I like to be enabled."

1. What did you notice about this video segment? What are your initial reactions?
2. Does Juan accept Lazarus's version of an appropriate treatment plan?
3. Where would Juan and Lazarus go from here in order to develop an appropriate treatment formulation?

B. Watch the following video segment as Jon Carlson works with Gina to develop a possible direction for therapy.

START: "It's almost selfish to a fault, it sounds like . . ." STOP: "and I'm sorry for that part of our relationship."

1. What did you notice about this video segment? What are your initial reactions?
2. What is it that Carlson suggests that Gina consider?
3. Does Gina accept Carlson's suggestions?
4. Where would Gina and Carlson go from here in order to develop an appropriate treatment formulation?

C. Watch the following video segment as Len Sperry works to develop a mutual understanding of Kathleen's case formulation.

START: "There is gonna be three possible answers . . ." "If you could get that answer tonight and be absolutely certain . . ." STOP: "I really don't know off-hand."

1. What did you notice about this video segment? What are your initial reactions?
2. How does Sperry attempt to elicit Kathleen's case formulation?
3. What does Sperry learn about Kathleen during this segment?
4. Where would Sperry go from here in order to elicit a better understanding of Kathleen's formulation?

D. Watch the following segment as Len Sperry continues to work with Kathleen and then discusses the development of his formulation.

START: "Let me ask you something else. Could you demonstrate what that tightness is like . . ." "So I if was to come into the room . . . how would I see you?" Continue with the conversation where Len explains . . . STOP: "This is what this particular segment is telling me."

1. What did you notice about this segment? What are your initial reactions?
2. Why would Sperry have asked the client to demonstrate her symptoms nonverbally?
3. How was this segment useful for the therapist?

Chapter 6

A. Watch the following video segment as Len Sperry works with Kathleen and demonstrates assessment of symptomatic distress.

START: "But I was fine that day . . ." "What do you think accounts for that?" STOP: "Is that kind of an ironclad rule . . ." "Yeah." START: "How do they usually come on?" "And about how long would they hold?" "And when was the last one / and when was the first one?" STOP: "anything quite that intense" ". . . I just get all stressed out"

1. What did you notice about these video segments? What are your initial reactions?
2. How does Sperry elicit the client's understanding of what triggers her symptoms?
3. How is this information useful to the therapist?
4. How does Sperry discover this client's symptomatic manifestations?
5. What biological manifestations does this client experience?
6. What cognitive manifestations does this client experience?
7. What behavioral manifestations does this client experience?
8. Describe the intensity of this client's symptoms.
9. How does this information contribute to the therapist's development of a focused assessment?

Chapter 7

A. Automatic thoughts are often distorted perceptions of self. Watch the following video segment as Richard Stuart works with Wesley and Adel.

START: "How are you in your eyes now?" STOP: "And I don't know if I'll ever be satisfied with myself."

1. What did you notice about this video segment? What are your initial reactions?
2. What is the negative belief that this client holds about herself?

3. How does the therapist identify this belief?
4. Do you think the client believes that this belief is distorted?
5. How might a therapist help this client work with this belief?

B. Watch the following video segment as Richard Stuart explains how Wesley's words or behaviors trigger Adel's distorted thinking patterns.

START: "When you hear him say that I'm not sure I'm going to be with you" "You are telling her she's fat . . ." STOP: "Yeah, I understand that."

1. What did you notice in this video segment? What are your initial reactions?
2. How do Adel's automatic thoughts affect her relationship with Wesley?
3. How do automatic thoughts interfere with how individuals process information?

C. Watch the following video segment as Richard Stuart shares a personal example of how behaviors can affect feelings.

START: "I've gotta tell you a story" STOP: "like you've got your own private joke."

1. What did you notice in this video segment? What are your initial reactions?
2. What is Stuart suggesting in this segment?
3. What is the relationship between feelings, thoughts, and behaviors?

D. Watch the following segment as Richard Stuart explains the concept of "acting as if."

START: "I've got to get over the idea that I'm gonna get hurt again" STOP: "It's not gonna happen unless you act as if you've got it"

1. What did you notice in this video segment? What are your initial reactions?
2. Explain the concept of "acting as if."
3. How does this concept apply to the use of cognitive-behavioral interventions?

E. Social skills training methods are employed by therapists to help clients learn the necessary skills to improve their functioning. Watch the following video segment as Gus Napier demonstrates modeling of assertive behavior.

START: "So you are frustrated . . . did you hear his response . . . can I interrupt you though . . . there is also a parental part of that" STOP: "I know it feels like I'm taking his side here, but this is a life or death situation."

1. What did you notice about this video segment? What are your initial reactions?
2. How does Napier demonstrate modeling?
3. How does Napier demonstrate the use of assertiveness?
4. Why is this social skill so important for this client?

Chapter 8

A. Watch the following video segment as James Bitter demonstrates the use of open-ended verbalizations and gentle commands.

START: "Tell me how a typical day goes at your house?" STOP: "Well I just have to keep calling them and calling them."

1. What did you notice about this video segment? What are your initial reactions?

2. How did Bitter use a gentle command? What did he say?

3. How effective was this technique?

4. Why would Bitter want to know about the families typical day? How is that information helpful to the therapist?

B. Watch the following video segment as O'Hanlon demonstrates the use of clarifying skills

START: "And if you didn't get her going would she get to work? But she gets herself up . . . wait a minute—there is a crack in your story here." STOP: "She gets herself up and goes to work."

1. What did you notice about this video segment? What are your initial reactions?

2. How did O'Hanlon clarify Adrian's and Judy's assumption that Pam never does anything on her own?

3. What information did the family leave out?

4. Why is this information important?

5. How effective is this technique?

C. Watch the following video segment as Berg demonstrates confronting discrepancies and incongruencies.

START: "Was it hard on Sunday? . . . Are you that kind of person that has strong will?" STOP: "One thing I really dislike about myself is that I let my emotions take control."

1. What did you notice about this video segment? What are your initial reactions?

2. How did Berg demonstrate confronting skills?

3. What incongruence do you think Berg picked up on?

4. How do you think the client may have been inconsistent?

5. How effective is this technique?

D. Watch the following video segment as Hardy demonstrates the use of therapeutic confrontational skills.

START: "And what is your understanding of why you lie? It doesn't seem to me that you have had the opportunity . . . that you are compromising yourself . . . as a way of warding off criticism, that that tactic only invites the only thing that you are trying . . . it seems like you have gotten a lot of that . . . and you . . ." STOP: "And I just think that must be a very torturous way to live one's life."

1. What did you notice about this video segment? What are your initial reactions?

2. What specific confrontational skills did Hardy demonstrate?

3. How did Hardy confront a discrepancy occurring in Phil's life?

4. Why do you think this technique is useful?

E. Watch the following video segment where Hardy continues to work with Phil and establishes connections between his thoughts and behaviors.

START: "Could you imagine yourself saying to her . . . and do your feelings go away? Because I keep sensing that they don't. No, they don't . . . ." STOP: "It's all those things you're throwing up all those things."

1. What did you notice about this video segment? What are your initial reactions?

2. How effective did Hardy establish connections between fills thoughts, behaviors, and the results he experiences?

3. How do you think this technique impacted Phil?

4. Why do you think this technique is useful?

Chapter 9

A. Watch the video segment as Frank Pittman demonstrates the use of curricular questioning.

START: "So what do you do when Susan is talking about herself?" STOP: ". . . what I need to do in the immediate future."

1. What do you notice about how Pittman phrases the question?
2. What do you notice about how the client responds to the question either verbally or nonverbally?
3. How effective do you think this question was in this particular segment?
4. Under what circumstances could you imagine yourself using this technique?

B. Watch the video segment as Insoo Kim Berg demonstrates the use of reflective questioning.

START: "So suppose that you were able to do that" STOP: "She's handling it, ok."

1. What do you notice about how Berg phrases the question?
2. What do you notice about how the client responds to the question either verbally or nonverbally?
3. How effective do you think this question was in this particular segment?
4. Under what circumstances could you imagine yourself using this technique?

C. Watch the video segment as Jon Carlson demonstrates the use of strategic questioning.

START: "So it sounds like there is another thing that the two of you have . . . well if it's with the right person . . . is it with the right person or being the right person" STOP: "She's gonna have her opinion and I'm gonna have mine."

1. What do you notice about how Carlson phrases the question?
2. What do you notice about how the client responds to the question either verbally or nonverbally?
3. How effective do you think this question was in this particular segment?
4. Under what circumstances could you imagine yourself using this technique?

D. Watch the video segment as Steve Madigan demonstrates the use of externalizing questions.

START: "What else would happen to you if you developed a troubled reputation . . . . " STOP: "Then I'll be in a whole lotta trouble."

1. What do you notice about how Madigan phrases the question?
2. What do you notice about how the client responds to the question either verbally or nonverbally?
3. How effective do you think this question was in this particular segment?
4. Under what circumstances could you imagine yourself using this technique?

E. Watch the video segment as Jon Carlson demonstrates the use of empowering questions.

START: "So what could you guys do . . . I'm getting the feeling that you guys are the kind of people . . . who are gonna do it . . ." STOP: "Well she mentioned me joining a bowling league."

1. What do you notice about how Carlson phrases the question?

2. What do you notice about how the client responds to the questions either verbally or nonverbally?
3. How effective do you think this question was in this particular segment?
4. Under what circumstances could you imagine yourself using this technique?

F. Watch the video segment as Jon Carlson demonstrates the use of scaling questions.

START: "Are you more up or are you more down these days?" STOP: "So these are really good days for you."

1. What do you notice about how Carlson phrases the question?
2. What do you notice about how the client responds to the question either verbally or nonverbally?
3. How effective do you think this question was in this particular segment?
4. Under what circumstances could you imagine yourself using this technique?

G. Watch the video segment as O'Hanlon demonstrates the use of exception questions.

START: "I'm really interested in . . . tell me about a moment when it seems to go better . . . what happens then? What is different? So give me an example of a time when you did something on your own, you just did it . . ." STOP: "What did you do different?"

1. What do you notice about how O'Hanlan phrases the question?
2. What do you notice about how the client responds to the question either verbally or nonverbally?
3. How effective do you think this question was in this particular segment?
4. Under what circumstances could you imagine yourself using this technique?

H. Watch the video segment as Steve Madigan demonstrates the use of positive description questions.

START: "Which would you prefer to have, a good boy reputation or a bad boy reputation?" STOP: "If you have a trouble reputation you wouldn't have many friends."

1. What do you notice about how Madigan phrases the questions?
2. What do you notice about how the client responds to the questions either verbally or nonverbally?
3. How effective do you think these questions were in this particular segment?
4. Under what circumstances could you imagine yourself using this technique?

I. Watch the video segment as Insoo Kim Berg demonstrates the use of outcome questions.

START: "How will you know that coming in here was a good idea . . . what would be different? . . . How will that be helpful for you?" STOP: "I'd be much more calm."

1. What do you notice about how Berg phrases the question?
2. What do you notice about how the client responds to the question either verbally or nonverbally?
3. How effective do you think this question was in this particular segment?
4. Under what circumstances could you imagine yourself using this technique?

J. Watch the video segment as Cheryl Rampage demonstrates the use of coping questions.

START: "I guess I've just been a lot more stressed out lately?" "What are you doing for yourself being stressed out right now . . . ." STOP: ". . . what do you imagine would be helpful?"

1. What do you notice about how Rampage phrases the question?
2. What do you notice about how the client responds to the question either verbally or nonverbally?
3. How effective do you think this question was in this particular segment?
4. Under what circumstances could you imagine yourself using this technique?

Chapter 10

A. Structural Family Therapists focus on helping families develop boundaries and appropriate hierarchies. Watch the following video segment as Aponte demonstrates this in his work with Judy (mother) and Pam (daughter).

START: Aponte: "You guys take very good care of this young woman but she needs to do more for herself . . . what I am suggesting . . . you can show her how you can still take good care of her and she can still grow up." START: Aponte: "See I think what's happening in your relationship is . . ." END: with Aponte: ". . . she loses that little bit of having a mother."

1. What did you notice about this video segment? What are your initial reactions?
2. How does this segment demonstrate the use of structural interventions?
3. What specific structural techniques did you notice Aponte use in this segment?
4. What are some of the suggestions Aponte offers to Judy?
5. How might those suggestions lead to the development of stronger boundaries/hierarchies?

B. During the video session, Aponte discovers a strong alliance between Pam and her father, Adrian, but notices a great deal of tension between Pam and Judy. Watch as Aponte works with this family using structural interventions.

START: Mother: "She'll work with him more than she will with me." Aponte: "Why is that, Adrian?" STOP: with Aponte: "If you stay with it, it will work. I think you already know what works."

1. What did you notice about this video segment? What are your initial reactions?
2. How and why does Aponte attempt to restructure this particular family dynamic?
3. How does this segment demonstrate the use of structural interventions?
4. What specific structural techniques did you notice Aponte use in this segment?
5. Discuss the interplay of alliances, hierarchies, and subsystems.

C. During the video session, Philip Guerin demonstrates the use of structural interventions with Pam, Judy, and Adrian.

START: "Do you think Pam has as good of a relationship with you as she does with your wife?" STOP: "Are the two of them in a conspiracy to avoid having you tell them what to do?" Everyone laughs.

1. What did you notice about this segment? What are your initial reactions?
2. What does Guerin notice about the relationship between Pam, Judy, and Adrian?
3. How would you characterize the relationships in this family based on this segment?
4. What specific techniques does Guerin use to work with this family?

D. START: "What would happen if you won a lottery and part of it was that you won a condo ..." STOP: "So everybody ought to just leave you alone with it."

5. What did you notice about this segment? What are your initial reactions?
6. What does Guerin notice about the relationship between Pam, Judy, and Adrain?
7. How would you characterize the relationships in this family based on this segment?
8. What specific techniques does Guerin use to work with this family?

Chapter 11

A. Watch the following video segment as G. Alan Marlatt works with Danny to develop a therapeutic alliance.

START: "So once you realized you were hooked ..." "a couple times I got off because I was hanging out ..." "But you did that by yourself ..." "How long was the withdrawal ..." "How did you keep from using during that time?" STOP: "You got back into it again." START: "So what do you look forward to if you ..." STOP: "All you've got to do is take that first step."

1. What did you notice about these video segments? What are your initial reactions?
2. What questions does Marlatt ask to help him understand this particular client's perspective?
3. What does Marlatt discover about this client's personal resources?
4. What does Marlatt discover about this client's motivation for change?
5. What does Marlatt discover about this client's barriers to treatment?
6. How does this information help a therapist in tailoring a treatment program?
7. How does this information help a therapist in anticipating non-adherence?

B. Watch the following clip as Marlatt continues to work with Danny.

START: "It doesn't sound like you ... so it's a friend ... so how do you break up with this friend? If you were to say good bye to heroin ... so it's funny you are not really angry at it." STOP: "If I get mad at anybody it would be myself."

1. What did you notice about this video segment? What are your initial reactions?
2. What technique does Marlatt use to elicit an understanding of the client's acceptance of responsibility?
3. How can this understanding help a therapist work with a client to prevent relapse?

Chapter 12

A. It is essential to consider cultural factors when building therapeutic relationships. Watch the following video segment as Jon Carlson and Mary Arnold work with a couple and consider their cultural context in an initial therapy session.

START: Arnold: "I'm curious about something..." STOP: with Arnold and client: "Behind every great man there is a woman pushing." "An Irish woman?" "Pushing," START: Arnold: "So it works for an Irish women who is used to pushing but it doesn't work for a Polish man who feels dominated. So we have to kind of work with that." END. START: Arnold: "You two are really working against some very heavy cultural messages..." END: with Arnold: "... she's gonna push harder."

1. What did you notice in this video segment? What are your initial reactions?
2. How does understanding an individual's, couple's, or family's culture help the therapist to work more effectively?
3. How does the cultural backgrounds of the couple in the video influence their relationship?
4. Are there any common themes between Martha and John and their respective cultures?

B. Initial greetings vary among therapists. Some therapists choose to open an initial session by allowing the client to ask any questions they might have. Watch the following video segment as Lenore Walker begins an initial session with Gina.

START: (at very beginning) STOP: "and then I'll kind of give you a little feedback at the end and let you know what I see that's going on."

1. What did you notice about this video segment? What are your initial reactions?
2. How do you think Gina responded to Walker's initial comments?
3. How do you see yourself opening an initial therapeutic interview?

C. When concluding an initial interview the therapist often briefly summarizes what was covered in the therapy session or offers suggestions to the client. Watch the following video segments as Insoo Kim Berg and Arnold Lazarus demonstrate closing an initial therapy session.

START: Lazarus: "One thing I want to come back to and end with..." "What grade would I receive?" STOP: "Take care."
START: Berg: "I have some suggestions for you to experiment with." STOP: "I wish you luck—thank you very much"

1. What did you notice about these video segments? What are your initial reactions?
2. How do the clients seem to respond to Lazaru's summary and closing of the session?
3. How do the clients seem to respond to Berg's summary and closing of the session?
4. What suggestions does Lazarus offer to his client?
5. What suggestions does Berg offer to her client?
6. What is different and what is similar about Lazarus's and Berg's closings?

Answer Key

Chapter 1

True and False Questions
1. F, 2. F, 3. T, 4. F, 5. F, 6. T, 7. F, 8. T, 9. T, 10. F, 11. T, 12. T

Multiple Choice Questions
1. D, 2. C, 3. B, 4. A, 5. C, 6. D, 7. B, 8. B, 9. D, 10. A, 11. E, 12. D

Chapter 2

True and False Questions
1. F, 2. F, 3. F, 4. T, 5. F, 6. F, 7. T, 8. T, 9. T, 10. T

Multiple Choice Questions
1. B, 2. B, 3. B, 4. C, 5. C, 6. C, 7. B, 8. C, 9. B, 10. A

Chapter 3

True and False Questions
1. T, 2. T, 3. T, 4. F, 5. F, 6. T, 7. T, 8. F, 9. F, 10. T

Multiple Choice Questions
1. C, 2. A, 3. E, 4. C, 5. C, 6. D, 7. A, 8. D, 9. B, 10. B

Chapter 4

True and False Questions
1. F, 2. F, 3. T, 4. T, 5. F, 6. T, 7. F, 8. F

Multiple Choice Questions
1. D, 2. C, 3. D, 4. C, 5. E, 6. B, 7. E, 8. E

Chapter 5

True and False Questions
1. T, 2. T, 3. F, 4. F, 5. F, 6. T, 7. F, 8. T

Multiple Choice Questions
1. B, 2. C, 3. B, 4. B, 5. D, 6. A, 7. C, 8. C

Chapter 6

True and False Questions
1. F, 2. F, 3. F, 4. T, 5. F, 6. F, 7. T, 8. T

Multiple Choice Questions
1. D, 2. C, 3. B, 4. C, 5. E, 6. A, 7. B, 8. D, 9. E, 10. D

Chapter 7

True and False Questions
1. T, 2. T, 3. T, 4. F, 5. T, 6. F, 7. F, 8. T, 9. T, 10. F

Multiple Choice Questions
1. D, 2. C, 3. B, 4. A, 5. C, 6. D, 7. D, 8. D, 9. B, 10. D

Chapter 8

True and False Questions
1. F, 2. F, 3. T, 4. T, 5. T, 6. F, 7. T, 8. T, 9. T, 10. T

Multiple Choice Questions
1. D, 2. C, 3. B, 4. D, 5. A, 6. B, 7. B, 8. D, 9. D, 10. B

Chapter 9

True and False Questions
1. T, 2. T, 3. T, 4. C, 5. F, 6. T, 7. T, 8. F, 9. T, 10. T

Multiple Choice Questions
1. D, 2. C, 3. B, 4. C, 5. A, 6. B, 7. A, 8. D, 9. C, 10. B

Chapter 10

True and False Questions
1. T, 2. F, 3. T, 4. F, 5. T, 6. T, 7. F, 8. T, 9. T, 10. F

Multiple Choice Questions
1. D, 2. D, 3. C, 4. C, 5. C, 6. A, 7. D, 8. B, 9. A, 10. B

Chapter 11

True and False Questions
1. T, 2. F, 3. T, 4. T, 5. F, 6. T, 7. F, 8. T, 9. T, 10. F

Multiple Choice Questions
1. B, 2. D, 3. D, 4. C, 5. E, 6. D, 7. D, 8. E, 9. A, 10. B

Chapter 12

True and False Questions
1. F, 2. F, 3. T, 4. F, 5. T, 6. F, 7. T, 8. F, 9. T, 10. T

Multiple Choice Questions
1. B, 2. B, 3. E, 4. D, 5. D, 6. C, 7. C, 8. B, 9. D, 10. D

References

Carlson, J. and Kjos, D. (1998). *Structural Therapy with Harry Aponte*. Boston: Allyn & Bacon.

Carlson, J. and Kjos, D. (1998). *Solution Focused Therapy with Insoo Kim Berg*. Boston: Allyn & Bacon.

Carlson, J. and Kjos, D. (1998). *Adlerian Family Therapy with James Bitter*. Boston: Allyn & Bacon.

Carlson, J. and Kjos, D. (1998). *Existential Humanistic Therapy with James Bugentàl*. Boston: Allyn & Bacon.

Carlson, J. and Kjos, D. (1998). *Adlerian Therapy with Jon Carlson*. Boston: Allyn & Bacon.

Carlson, J. and Kjos, D. (1998). *Culture-Sensitive Therapy with Jon Carlson and Mary Arnold*. Boston: Allyn & Bacon.

Carlson, J. and Kjos, D. (1998). *Bowenian Family Therapy with Phil Guerin*. Boston: Allyn & Bacon.

Carlson, J. and Kjos, D. (1998). *Family Systems Therapy with Ken Hardy*. Boston: Allyn & Bacon.

Carlson, J. and Kjos, D. (1998). *Multimodal Therapy with Arnold Lazarus*. Boston: Allyn & Bacon.

Carlson, J. and Kjos, D. (1998). *Narrative Therapy with Steve Madigan*. Boston: Allyn & Bacon.

Lewis, J. and Carlson, J. (2000). *Harm Reduction Therapy for Addictions with Alan Marlatt*. Boston: Allyn & Bacon.

Carlson, J. and Kjos, D. (1998). *Experiential Therapy with Gus Napier*. Boston: Allyn & Bacon.

Carlson, J. and Kjos, D. (1998). *Solution Oriented Therapy with Bill O'Hanlon*. Boston: Allyn & Bacon.

Carlson, J. and Kjos, D. (1998). *Empowerment Therapy with Frank Pittman*. Boston: Allyn & Bacon.

Carlson, J. and Kjos, D. (1998). *Feminist Therapy with Cheryl Rampage*. Boston: Allyn & Bacon.

Carlson, J. and Kjos, D. (1998). *Object Relations Therapy with Jill and David Scharff*. Boston: Allyn & Bacon.

Carlson, J. and Kjos, D. (2000). *Deactivating Psychosomatic Symptoms with Len Sperry*. Phoenix: Zeig Tucker & Co.

Carlson, J. and Kjos, D. (1998). *Behavioral Therapy with Richard Stuart*. Boston: Allyn & Bacon.